What Made Sammy Run?
My Story

By Sam Silberberg

Adapted for Young Adults by Carolyn Buan

Dedication

To you, my young readers—
may my story inspire you
to oppose acts of hatred
against your fellow human beings
wherever you find them.

Contents

Acknowledgments

Ever since I began to toy with the idea of writing about my childhood during the Holocaust in Poland, I have been amazed at the amount of interest my story has aroused and the offers of help I have received. Foremost among those I must thank is John Miller of Portland, Oregon, who accompanied me when I returned to Poland in 2000 and encouraged me to write my memoirs.

All along, I thought I was writing a book for adults—and, indeed, I have now published an adult version of my story entitled *From Hell to the Promised Land*. But meanwhile a friend of John's, Carolyn Buan, read my manuscript and thought there might be other possibilities. She and John met with Judy Margles, Museum Director of the Oregon Jewish Museum, who said, "Why don't you make this a book for young adults?" So with John's continued involvement, Judy's excellent suggestions and Carolyn's writing and editorial skills, *What Made Sammy Run?* was born. Another Portlander, Phyllis Moore, herself an editor with a longstanding involvement with my memoirs, agreed to lay out the present book following the suggestions of graphic designer Jeanne Galick, who also designed the cover. My sincerest thanks to all of these individuals for their fine work.

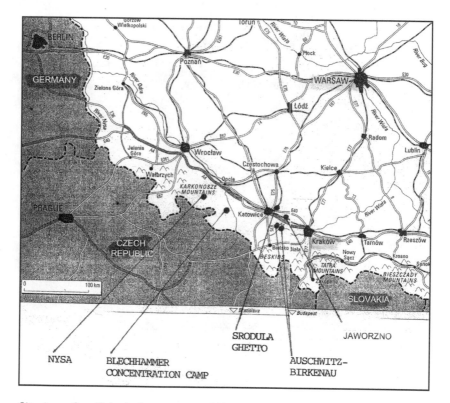

Sites in southern Poland where my story unfolds.

Hello,
My Name Is Sam

Hello. My name is Sam Silberberg. I'm an old guy—83 this year—so I'll bet you're wondering why I've decided to write a book for teenagers.

Well, you see, I've been thinking a lot about my own youth, when I was about your age and younger, and I realize that we have a lot in common.

Oh, I didn't grow up where you did. I lived in a small town in Poland, in Eastern Europe. If you'd known me then, you wouldn't have called me Sam, you'd have called me Shmilek, which is like Sammy in English. In fact, you might not have liked me. I was a skinny, feisty kid, who always took a lot of chances. It must have driven my parents nuts.

But, then, that was a time when we all lived in great danger, and you had to take chances. You see, I grew up during the 1930s and 40s, when Germany was determined to seize every country in the world, starting in Europe. And my home in Poland was very close to Germany.

The other thing you need to know about me is that I come from a Jewish family, and Jews were anything but popular.

So how should I start telling you this story of mine? I have to say, I've given this question a lot of thought. In the end, I've decided it's probably best just to begin at the beginning. You know—"I was born on [fill in the date] in [fill in the place]." Yes, I'll do that.

Oh, I know what you're thinking. This guy's an old man who will probably have trouble remembering his childhood. But there you'd be wrong. Even after 70-some years, every detail of my childhood is burned into my brain. You'll soon see why.

So let's go back to my early life. I want you to come with me. You'll be right beside me when I'm a little kid in Poland in the 1930s, and you'll be there in September 1939 when I'm 10 and the Germans invade our town, seize our homes and businesses and send us away to live in crowded Jewish ghettos. You'll be there when the Germans catch my cousin and me and put us in prison but we escape. You'll stand in the public square the day our family is suddenly torn apart and shipped off to different concentration camps, with no real chance to say goodbye. You'll be with my father and me in those camps and on the final death march. And we'll go together and fight in the Holy Land to establish the country of Israel for the Jewish people. Oh, you'll see what my life was like all right.

First Things First

As my story begins, I have just celebrated my eighth birthday. I was born on August 25, 1929 in Jaworzno, Poland, a coal-mining town with a population of 25,000. (I want you to pronounce it properly – it's *Ya-VORZ-No*.) Of the 25,000 residents, only about 1,600 of us are Jewish. Most of the rest are Catholics, and I can assure you they don't like us Jews very much.

My father and mother are very strict orthodox Jews, who observe all the religious traditions of Chasidic (or Hasidic) Judaism. I'll tell you more about those traditions later on.

As my story begins, my extended family in Jaworzno and the surrounding towns consists of 108 people, whose history in this area stretches back many generations. Recently, all 108 of us gathered to celebrate the wedding of my Aunt Sarah. What a crazy party that was— and how happy was the bride!

But more about our background.

The Silberberg clan is very hard working. My grandfather owns a print shop and a stationery store and is a majority stockholder in the family bus company, which services the area between the cities of Katowice (*Cat-o-VE-chay*) in the west and Krakow (*CRACK-ov*) in the east. He and Grandmother had nine children—five boys and four girls, all of whom are now grown and actively involved in the family businesses.

My father and mother own a clothing store, and my father works nights in the family print shop. Mother is always busy helping Father in the business, so until I had my third birthday I was nursed and raised by Julka, our Christian nanny. At that tender age, I began to attend cheder, an orthodox Jewish religious school, from 9:00 a.m. to 4:00 p.m., with a break for lunch. There I began to learn to read Hebrew prayer books and the Jewish holy book, the Torah. After my sixth birthday I started to attend public school from 8:30 to 12:30 and cheder from 1:30 to 4:30. That keeps me very busy all week, and on the weekend– from sundown on Friday to sundown on Saturday–we celebrate the Hebrew Sabbath.

First my father takes us to a Turkish bath, and we get dressed in our holiday outfits. Then we go to prayer services at the synagogue. After that, we visit my great-grandmother, who is always seated at the head of a long table covered with a white tablecloth, surrounded by the entire Silberberg clan. After her oldest son makes the Kiddush, a prayer, she distributes candies to all of her great-grandchildren and everyone returns to their homes for the Sabbath meal.

That's enough background for you. Now come along with me. I have adventures in store for both of us.

It is the last week in August 1937, the week of my birthday. My mother, my two brothers, my sister and our nanny are just returning home from our vacation in the mountains so that Mother can get us outfitted for school. At age 6½ my sister, Ruzia (Rachel in English), is just starting school, while my older brother, Moniek (Moses David), age 12, is beginning his first year in high school. My younger brother, Ben-Zion (the Son of Zion, nicknamed Benek), is 5 and attends the Hebrew school.

So what can I tell you about my brothers and sister? Well, Rachel loves to talk, and as little as she is she already wants to work in our parents' shop. She's kind of a little miss know-it-all, so she'd probably drive the customers batty. Rachel has a sharp little chin so we call her *Gempka*, which means just that–sharp chin. She knows it's a term of endearment so she doesn't mind.

Four generations of the Silberberg family attend Aunt Sarah's wedding

My big brother Moses David is four and a half years older than me and is a real bookworm. Oh, I pay attention in school and do my homework, but when the school day is over I want to be out climbing trees and playing with my friends. Not Moses David. He's the brainy one. He has sandy hair, blue eyes and a long face. (That's not a criticism—it's just the truth!)

My brother Benek is second from the left in this photo. I am the tall boy in the second row, then known as Shmilek. No photos of Moses David or Rachel survived the war.

5

Little Benek has black hair and eyes that are sort of green. People say he's a beautiful boy, and he's strong. The only thing that's odd about him is his voice: it always sounds like he's talking through his nose. That's because of an accident he had. Benek is also talented with his hands. He loves to take things apart, and he always figures out how to put them back together again.

You'll get to know my parents better later on. Right now I'll just say that my father is a very fine man, who is looked up to by everybody in our synagogue. And Mother, with her coal-black hair and blue eyes, has always been considered a beauty. When she was a little girl, she was once chosen to present a bouquet of flowers to Kaiser Franz Joseph when he came to visit. In those days you were chosen to present flowers to important people partly because you were pretty.

The end of summer vacation is an especially hectic time for my mother. In addition to getting us ready for school, she has to help my father in our clothing store, where they are very busy selling new school outfits for children. And she must prepare everything for the celebration of Rosh Hashanah (the Jewish New Year) and the Jewish

My mother, Baila Siegman Silberberg, and my father, Solomon Silberberg.

6

high holy days, which start by mid-September. Meanwhile, I hook up with friends from my schools to find out how they spent their summer vacations and get updated on the latest events in town.

What I learn from them is very exciting. During the second week of September, the Polish army will conduct maneuvers in town with all sorts of military equipment, and us kids can watch. We have a few days left before the maneuvers begin, so we spend most of our time playing various war games in the yards of our families and friends.

It's one day before Rosh Hashanah, and the maneuvers have started. My friends and I have followed the tanks and armored vehicles into the fields to watch them play their war games.

Suddenly, I feel a horrible pain in my belly. I try to ignore it, hoping that it will disappear, but it's getting worse and I have to go home to bed. When my mother sees me writhing in bed instead of watching the maneuvers, she realizes that I must really be in pain. I am in *so much* pain, in fact, that I can't go to the synagogue for Rosh Hashanah or join the family at dinner.

I have a sleepless night, and in the morning my mother goes to the garden and picks some large green leaves to use with ice as a compress on my belly, but it doesn't help. As I keep moaning and groaning, my mother goes to fetch the doctor. He tells her that I have a ruptured appendix and must be taken to a hospital in Krakow, which is about 50 kilometers (36 miles) away.

Mother sends our nanny to the synagogue to get my father, who is performing the mid-day prayer service. He has to excuse himself from the worshipers and rush us to the bus terminal.

When we get to the hospital, we are told that my ruptured appendix is so far gone the doctor can't guarantee the success of the operation. We also learn that I must stay in the hospital for a very long time and have wads of cotton soaked with pus pulled out of a large incision in my belly over and over again.

I don't know how long I have been here. Mostly I sleep. Once, as I wake up, I see my grandfather by my bedside, praying and reciting the Psalms of David for my successful recovery.

The Gathering Clouds
of War

It is the fall of 1938 and the family is throwing a large going-away party for my grandfather, who is leaving Poland for Palestine, where he will live in Jerusalem, in the "Promised Land." The celebration is joyful, but the mood is solemn. People are standing around in circles discussing "things" in hushed tones. I'm not supposed to be eavesdropping on adult conversations, but I can sense that something is very wrong.

I soon find out that the topic of greatest concern is the persecution of Jews in Germany. The German leader, Adolph Hitler, is determined to get rid of the Jewish population, and his goons have been conducting raids, breaking windows in shops owned by Jews (on Krystal Nacht, or the Night of Broken Glass), killing Jews and destroying their property. Also, these Nazis forbid Jews to send their children to school or gather in public or practice their professions, and they have shut down the Jewish newspapers. So now, people here in Poland are afraid the persecutions will spread to neighboring countries like ours. This alarms me, because every day at school I already feel the hatred other Poles have for us Jews.

In public school, where the majority of pupils are Catholic, we Jewish kids are constantly harassed and called Jew bastard, Christ killer, Jew Leper. When I first informed my father about this bullying, he told me the story of Christ's Crucifixion 2,000 years ago and assured me that the Jews are not to blame for it. He told me that the attitudes of these kids stem from the teaching of their parents and the Catholic Church, who hold the Jewish people responsible for killing Christ. I guess they've forgotten that Christ himself was a Jew!

I told my father that I resent being hassled over something that happened that long ago—something I had nothing to do with. When it comes right down to it, though, as long as the abuse I have to put up with is verbal, I don't mind. (You know what they say: *Sticks and stones may break my bones, but words can never hurt me.*) But one day the Polish kids started to beat up on me and my friends, and I decided to fight back. I invited some of the Jewish kids to gather in my house, which is near the school, so we could walk there together. I let the Polish kids know that I wasn't afraid to fight them. Later, they nicknamed me *grozny zydek* (the fearless Jew), which I didn't mind at all!

As I stand listening to the grownups, my face must be showing my fear, because my Uncle Moses notices me and takes me aside. He explains about what is happening to the Jews in Germany as if I were an adult and says, "If anything should happen here that leaves you stranded and alone, you must make your way through Europe to Turkey, and from there to Syria and on to Palestine, where you can join your grandfather." He explains that it is important for Jews to return to Zion and establish their own homeland, where they will not be persecuted.

Uncle Moses

(In case you aren't familiar with the term *Zion,* it refers to the ancestral land of the Jews, which is now the country of Israel. *Zionism* is a political movement that started at the end of the 1800s and urged Jews to resettle in Israel, where they could make their own laws and escape the persecution and massacres of their people that had taken place in Europe for centuries.

You see, long ago the Jews were forced to leave their homeland and spread out across Europe and beyond. The places where they were exiled are known as the "Diaspora." One of the ways these Jewish exiles were later persecuted was to have their land taken away and be told they couldn't own any land at all. That is why Jews couldn't become farmers and, instead, had to become merchants, bankers and middlemen to survive.)

My conversation with Uncle Moses has opened my eyes and ignited the first spark of yearning to go to the Holy Land and join the Zionist movement. He has shown me that I don't have to put up with insults and worse because I am Jewish. He has said that it is up to *us* to free ourselves from the yoke of persecution. He also said that my younger brother was named Ben-Zion to express our family's yearning and love for Zion. I am proud that Uncle Moses thinks I am mature enough to have a conversation like this even though I am only 9 years old.

A year has passed. It's the end of August, and we are back from our summer vacation and getting ready to start another school year. My parents are busy in the store selling new school outfits, the chestnut tree in the garden is dropping nuts, and the tomatoes are ready for picking.

Out in the streets the Polish army is conducting various maneuvers while, overhead, German planes are dropping chocolate bars and leaflets telling us Poles not to worry—they come in peace. But people say that the chocolate is laced with poison, and we are warned not to touch it.

Meanwhile, the Polish soldiers assure us that they wouldn't give up so much as a button from their uniforms to the Germans. Everything *appears* to be normal, but we *know* about Krystal Nacht, we *know* that the Germans have invaded Czechoslovakia and we wonder if Poland will be next.

Today is the first of September. In the darkness just before dawn, we are awakened by loud explosions. We rush to the windows facing the street and see spark-like objects whizzing past us and hear more explosions in the distance. To us children, it seems like a display of fireworks and we watch in fascination until our parents come up to the second floor and tell us how dangerous the situation is. "Stay away from the windows," they order as they quickly gather our belongings and start to pack.

Later, my father says he has ordered a horse and wagon to pick us up and take us eastward to the city of Krakow. This beautiful medieval city was the ancient capital of Poland, and Father thinks it will be protected from an invasion by the Germans. As soon as the wagon arrives, we load our belongings in a hurry and all four kids jump up behind my mother and the nanny, who are sitting in the front seat. My father will stay behind to keep a watchful eye on our home and store and on his father's home and print shop. Everything is so hectic we don't know if any of his brothers or his sister Goldie are leaving or staying in Jaworzno.

This is our house on Mickiewicza Street as it looked in 2000, when I went back to Poland for the first time since the end of World War II. Despite the many thousand miles I had traveled, the Polish family that lived in our house would not allow me inside. Unfortunately, hatred of Jews is still alive and well in Poland.

We say our goodbyes to our father and are on our way—down Mickiewicza (*Meech-ka-VE-cha*) Street, then left onto Jagielonska (*Yag-eg-LONCH-kah*) Street, which is the main road leading to Krakow.

There, the street is crowded with horse-drawn wagons and columns of military trucks and vehicles. We assume that the military vehicles are traveling to Krakow to take up defensive positions on the Wistula (*VIS-tu-lah*) River to protect the city from the German invaders.

All day we can hear the whizzing sound of bullets and the sound of explosions getting louder and closer. As the skies grow dark and night falls, we can see the traces of artillery fire (the fire from big, mounted guns) glowing in the dark skies. It reminds us of fireworks until we see a shell land on top of a horse-drawn wagon, severely injuring the people in it.

This is Friday night, the time we normally celebrate the Sabbath, or day of rest. Usually we would not be allowed to travel on this night, but it can't be helped. Mother wants to find a place in a village removed from the main road, where we can stay overnight and be sheltered from the artillery fire.

After numerous attempts she succeeds, but the place is cramped and uncomfortable. The plan is for us to stay in the village until Sunday morning and then continue on our way to Krakow, but the explosions keep us awake. By the time we settle into a deep sleep we are exhausted. In the morning we learn that the German army has already occupied Krakow.

Now we have no choice but to turn around and go back to Jaworzno. Because it is the Sabbath, Mother decides to stay in the village until Sunday morning. This gives us a chance to walk the 2 ½ kilometers (1½ miles) to the main road leading to Krakow and see for ourselves what is going on.

As we get closer to the road, we can hear the humming sound of German tanks and trucks loaded with soldiers. They are singing *Heute gehert uns Deutschland, morgen die gantze Welt!* (Today we own Germany, tomorrow the entire World!).

In the fall of 1939, German soldiers march into Warsaw, Poland, carrying bayonets. The invasion began on September 1 and plunged all of Europe into the Second World War. (United States Holocaust Memorial Museum, courtesy of National Archives and Records Administration, College Park)

Back in the village, we find that everyone is shocked by the defeat and the quick advance of the German army. Krakow, the center of Polish culture and civilization, has been overrun by German troops without anyone being able to stop them.

At the crack of dawn Sunday morning, we quickly pack our stuff and load it onto the wagon ready for the trip back to Jaworzno. As we enter the main road going east, we pass numerous columns of German military vehicles going the same direction, deeper into Poland. We are full of dread, wondering how our father has fared during our absence. There is very little traffic going our way, and yet it seems an eternity before we see the tall chimneys of the Jaworzno coal mines on the horizon.

On Jagielonska Street we pass the large bus garage our family owns. The streets here are deserted and the shutters on all the store windows are closed tight. As we turn right onto Mickiewicza Street past the school on the way to our house, my heart begins to race. The gate to our house is locked, and the store windows and door are shuttered.

Our wagon stops and my brother Moses David jumps down, taking a spare horseshoe with him. He starts knocking on the steel grating of the gate with the horseshoe, and only after continuous pounding does my father open the window of our second-floor bedroom. When he sees us, his face beams. Soon, he is opening the gate for the wagon to enter, and we are jumping down and hugging him with tears of joy and happiness because the family is together again.

Then we start to bombard him with questions: "How did things go in our absence? Why is everything so eerie and quiet?" He tells us that the German soldiers have been taking men (especially Jews) and using them as hostages to make sure that none of their soldiers are harmed. They announced in fliers distributed to the public that if any German soldier gets killed or injured, they would shoot and kill ten hostages. Now we understand why everyone is behind shuttered windows and doors: they are afraid of being arrested by the Germans.

The Noose Tightens

Several days have passed, and the Germans have gradually increased their grip on our lives by issuing restrictive decrees every day, telling us what we can and can't do. These decrees are posted on bulletin boards in the town square and the town hall. The Germans have imposed a dusk-to-dawn curfew, and anyone who violates it will be put to death. Hostages are taken daily in Jaworzno and neighboring towns. We recently got the sad news that in the town of Trzebinia (*Cha-BIN-yah*) between Jaworzno and Krakow, my father's brother, Uncle Maniek, was taken hostage and shot to death because shots were fired at a German outpost. He left a wife and two children, along with his printing plant, which now stands idle. The family is grief stricken and everyone is trying to find a way to help his widow survive the disaster that has befallen her.

While our whole family was still in mourning for Uncle Maniek, my father was taken hostage by the Germans. Because of Uncle Maniek's death, the entire family was panic stricken and the adults made frantic attempts to find out where he was being held in order to gain his release. Finally, after four painful days of constant contacts and a huge ransom, paid through a middleman, my father was released and is now home. I keep trying in various ways to find out what it took to get him released, but no one will tell me. All I know is that it took the pooling of money from all the branches of our family.

Since his release, my father looks different. We know that he was tortured and starved and had his beard shaven off, yet he refuses to discuss any details of his treatment in prison. With these experiences during the first week of the German occupation of Poland, we cannot help but wonder what is in store for us next.

The answer to that question appears during the second week in the form of new edicts announced on public bulletin boards. Every Jewish-owned business is to be put under the supervision of a German *Gauleiter* (Supervisor) appointed by the authorities. The business owners are accountable to this man for all financial transactions. No new merchandise can be obtained without his prior written approval, and sales records will be matched to the merchandise on hand twice a month. When the sales records and the merchandise don't match, the business owner will not be given more goods. Another new edict, effective October 1, 1939, decrees that all Jews must wear the yellow Star of David with the word *Jude* (Jew) inscribed on it. Any violation of these rules is punishable by deportation to a labor camp.

In spite of all these decrees, life in our community has gone on at a fairly normal pace. Public school has functioned as usual, except for the fact that gentile (non-Jewish) classmates will have nothing to do with us inside or outside of school for fear of being seen as too sympathetic to Jews. Also, some of the children whose parents are German belong to the organization *Hitler Jugend* (Youth for Hitler) and wear their German uniforms to school. Surprisingly, though, our Hebrew School has been allowed to function.

It is the spring of 1941, and over the past year everything has changed. New restrictive decrees are being announced every few days, making life very difficult. Yet it is amazing to see how creative people have been in getting around them. Since Jewish worship services require at least 10 men and many men would be afraid to attend synagogue, services are now held in the privacy of the worshipers' homes each week. The same system is being used to make sure that us kids continue to enjoy a good religious education. We are taught in various homes by teachers our parents have hired. To avoid making the authorities suspicious, we go to different homes each week.

Another year has passed and the Nazis have started to conduct raids to catch young, able-bodied Jewish men and send them off to concentration camps, where they are used by the Nazis as slave laborers. My older brother, Moses David, was caught in one of the raids and sent off to a concentration camp, but we don't know where he was taken. His absence has created a huge void in the family. We all miss him terribly and are constantly concerned about his fate.

As things get worse for our family, our parents no longer hide the truth from us. They make sure that we are aware of what is going on so that we don't get caught in a Nazi raid. We know, for example, that there is a concentration camp at Auschwitz (*OWSH-witz*), which is about 24 kilometers (15 miles) from Jaworzno. Another camp, Birkenau, (*BEER-ken-ow*) is right next to Auschwitz. All over Europe, Jews have been rounded up and taken there.

The stories we hear about these camps are horrifying. Auschwitz was originally built as a Polish officers' military compound, but Birkenau was designed by the Nazis and built by the inmates of Auschwitz. The Nazis raid Jewish areas in various European cities and force thousands of people into sealed cattle cars, where they stand for hours, packed in like sardines. The vents on these cars are covered with barbed wire and there are no toilets. You can imagine how foul smelling and disgusting they are.

Once a train is fully loaded, it is taken to Birkenau. There it stops near an enormous bathhouse, and Nazi officers with guard dogs force the people off the train. Everyone is ordered to leave their baggage and belongings behind because they are going to be cleaned and disinfected. They are told to take off their clothes and surrender all their valuables—they will get clean clothing when they are done with their showers. But the showers are connected to canisters of a poison called Zyklon-B. Once the showers are turned on, the poison is released. People scream and wail as they die, but no one can help them. Afterwards, their bodies are hauled to huge ovens, where they are burned.

Now, when we walk to and from the homes where we get our schooling, we have to make sure that our Polish neighbors don't see us and snitch to the Germans or we might end up in the camps. It is my duty to escort my younger sister and brother, so I have had to find clever ways to keep us hidden.

Once, not so long ago, I nearly got caught in a raid. It happened so quickly, my brother and sister barely had time to hide in a sealed-off room that my father had built in our basement behind a set of shelves. As soon as they were safely hidden, I ran upstairs to act as a lookout. At the front of our house is a double set of steel doors. I am skinny enough that I could hide between the left set of doors, while I kept the right set part way open.

Outside, I saw a Polish neighbor boy walk up to some German policemen and point out the entrance to our house. The Germans started walking towards it while the Polish boy waited to see what was going to happen.

The Germans walked through the right set of double doors within inches of where I was standing, but they didn't see me hiding in the shadows. As soon as they passed, I ran out, grabbed some stones, and hurled them at the Polish boy, who took off at top speed. Then I climbed the leafy chestnut tree in our yard and waited until the raid was over. This is the life we have gotten used to: surviving the raids.

One morning I had another experience that shook me up badly. I was in our clothing store, when I saw my Aunt Sarah walking up Jagielonska Street from the place where the bus from Krakow had let her off. She was dressed in a beige trench coat and her braided blond hair was pulled back in a style that made her look like a Polish woman, rather than a Jewish one. Her face was so filled with sadness, I could scarcely believe she was the same happy woman who had been married just a few years ago in front of 108 family members.

When she reached our store, where the family had gathered to greet her, we found out what had happened to make her so sad. The

Germans had destroyed the Jewish neighborhood where they lived in Krakow, and her husband and child had been taken to Auschwitz. She said that our Aunt Rachel, Rachel's husband, and their two children were taken, too. When we heard this, all of us burst into tears.

Now, my parents have learned that railroad cattle cars loaded with Jews are sitting on sidings at the Jaworzno train yards, waiting for their turn to enter the Birkenau death camp. During these layovers, my parents send me to the rail yards with bags of food and bottles of water. I am to throw the food and water through the barbed wire vents in the cattle cars for these poor, terrified people. For Jews, this is called doing a *mitzvah* (a good deed).

The first time I did this, I was afraid of the German guards who travel with the trains. I threw the food from a safe distance, but my aim was not good enough and the food fell to the ground outside the cars. In time, I got braver and managed to get close enough that the food I

Massive numbers of Jews being loaded into the cattle cars of trains bound for the concentration camps (Yad Vashem Photo Archives, courtesy of Robert A. Schmuhl, from the United States Holocaust Memorial Museum)

threw reached the prisoners' outstretched hands. As I got closer, I could also hear their agonizing cries and smell the dreadful stench of human waste coming from the cars. I can't tell you how terrible it was.

Now, each time I go, I am careful to hide in the bushes so that the German guards won't see me. If they ever catch me, they will throw me into one of those cattle cars and I will be on my way to the death camp.

Of course I've never told my parents how dangerous feeding the prisoners really is. If they knew, they would not allow me to do it again. I must admit, though, that I sometimes take big chances because I get a kick out of playing a cat-and-mouse game with the German guards and outsmarting them. In the process, I've learned several important evasion tactics.

Seeing the poor people in the rail cars and hearing their desperate cries has served as a strong warning to me: never will I allow myself to be trapped by the Germans nor will I give up hope. If you do that, you give up on life. But I am lucky: when my Uncle Moses told me to make my way to the Promised Land, he gave me something to live for.

I don't think that my family has any idea how angry my visits to the railroad yards have made me, and one day I was so infuriated that my anger boiled over. I said to my father, "Look, every year at Passover we say *Leshana Habaa B'Jerushalayim* (Next year we will be in Jerusalem). We've been saying it ever since I can remember. If instead of talking about it you had *taken* us there, we wouldn't be in danger now."

My father allowed me to blow off steam and then replied, "Would have, should have. We are in it now and we have to find a way to get out of it." Once I calmed down, of course, I realized that he was right: we have to cope with the mess we are in. Yet I get frustrated because sometimes – even at the age of 12 – I am *still* treated like a child. And I guess at 12 years of age, I *am*, because for Jewish boys the official passage into manhood doesn't take place until the age of 13, when boys celebrate their Bar Mitzvah, and I'm not quite there yet.

We Must Leave
Our Home Forever

It is May 1942 and today all of the bulletin boards in town have been covered with German posters that say **"Seven days from now Jaworzno must now be** *Juden Rein***"** (cleansed of Jews). This means that all of us must move out of our homes and businesses. We can move to the towns of Chrzanow (*CHA-noof*) or Sosnowiec (*Sos-NO-vietz*) and join the Jewish communities there.

Because Chrzanow is the county seat and my parents think Sosnowiec is a lower-class town, they say we will go to Chrzanow. But the fact that we only have seven days poses a problem for my father and his brothers. The Silberberg family donated the land for our synagogue, so they are responsible for all the religious objects that are kept there, as well as many family heirlooms and pieces of jewelry. These items would be hard to take with us, so the men have decided to hollow out some walls in my grandfather's house and our house and use them as hiding places.

My father let me watch the whole operation. The men opened the wall at Grandfather's house and buried the broken pieces they had removed. Then they carefully wrapped each of the items and placed them in the wall. When they were finished, Father patched the wall so carefully no one could ever tell it had been opened.

Next, Father did the same thing at our house, but the job was more involved because he had to work with stone masonry. Again, he did such a good job, it could fool anyone.

Leaving Jaworzno has caused enormous pain and hardship for our family. We have lost the money our store provided, as well as the income from our grandfather's print shop. And I may never see my friends again.

By the time we finished loading the wagon with our belongings, we realized that it is packed to the hilt and there was no room for us. So Father hired a horse-drawn taxi to take us to Chrzanow, which is 10 kilometers (6 ½ miles) away.

As we pulled away in the taxi, my sister Rachel started crying and shivering uncontrollably. She said she was terrified that we would never be able to enjoy the comforts of our own home again.

As it turns out, Rachel was right. Chrzanow is a town crowded with Jewish families who have been sent here from neighboring towns and villages, and we have not been able to find an apartment. Now we are living with our Aunt Esther (my father's sister), who moved here from Trzebinia, which was declared to be *Juden Rein* six months ago. Her husband was killed by the Germans as payback for an attack on a German military convoy by the Polish resistance movement.

This is a three-bedroom apartment that Aunt Esther and her two children, Janek and Shlomek, must now share with two more adults and three more children. It is so crowded that the children have to sleep on mattresses on the floor. But the apartment here has an indoor bathroom with running water to flush the toilet—a lot better than the outhouse we had in Jaworzno. Even so, if I had any choice, I would rather live in Jaworzno and use an outhouse than be under the crowded conditions here. But we no longer have a choice. Our lives are now governed by the whims and decrees of the German commanders, and who knows what cruel ones those evil men will come up with next.

When we are forced to move to Chrzanow, we move in with Father's sister, Aunt Esther, and her sons Janek (left) and Shlamek (right).

Even so, it never fails to amaze me how people can adapt and bounce back. In Chrzanow we have quickly adapted to a new routine. Aunt Esther has arranged for us to attend the same schools as her children. Now I am responsible for getting *four* children to school and making sure that we don't get caught in one of the German raids. I am not familiar with the area, so I have decided to spend my afternoons exploring and finding possible routes to use.

The Germans have summoned my father and ordered him to travel every day to Jaworzno and manage our store for them, but he is not allowed to stay over night there. Our home has been occupied by a Polish family that cooperates with the Nazis. My father must train these people to manage the business. They will use him for three months, but after that he is forbidden to return to Jaworzno or have any contact with any of his clients.

Despite being told that he must sever ties with his old clients, Father has been able to maintain some contacts and supply them with goods he gets on what is called the "black market." (Because the Germans have limited the amounts of food and other items that people can have, goods are obtained and secretly traded between Christians and Jews.)

Recently, I asked my parents to give me permission to trade on the black market and they did. But this has involved changing my appearance so that I can ride buses and streetcars. (We Jews are not allowed to use public transportation). First, my father trimmed my *peios* (side curls) and gave me a haircut. Then I had to find clothes that make me look like a Polish peasant or student, depending on where I go and what I do.

I have also had to develop new skills to avoid being detected by the Germans or snitched on by some Polish traitor who would like nothing better than to hand a Jew over to the Nazis. And, of course, I have had to learn the art of trading.

My father told me it is very simple. Really, he said, it boils down to supply and demand. You go to the Christian community and buy what the Jews need. Then you sell it to the Jews. You go to the Jewish community and buy what the Christians need and sell it to the Christians. Just start out with a few basic things. Peasants on the farm need clothing, shoes and other finished goods. Jews need food: bread, butter, eggs, milk and so on. You buy an item for two Deutsch marks

25

and sell it for three. Once you have done it several times, you will know exactly what to buy and how much to charge.

One more thing, Father warned me: you have to watch out so you are not caught by the German police while smuggling goods. He hardly needed to tell me *that*! But I have to admit that despite the dangers involved, I am thrilled with the game I am playing.

A New Edict—We Must Move to Sosnowiec

Wouldn't you know it? I've barely gotten used to life in Chrzanow and made some good trading contacts so I can help support our family, and the Germans have suddenly declared Chrzanow to be *Juden Rein*. All Jews must be ready to move to Sosnowiec—a much bigger city—within five days.

Father has already left for Sosnowiec to find an apartment for us before thousands of others arrive looking for places to live. He wants to find an apartment large enough to house five children and three adults.

Before leaving, he instructed us to pack only the most essential belongings and be ready to leave as soon as he returns. He said that he would hire two horse-drawn wagons for the move. As the oldest child, I have to keep the other four kids amused while my mother and Aunt Esther pack. Occasionally I am able to tear myself away from the children and help with the packing. Here, of course, we don't have much to take, so packing it up is a lot easier than it was when we left Jaworzno.

Father returned yesterday and informed us that he found a three-bedroom apartment in the Jewish quarter of Sosnowiec, which means we can beat the Germans' deadline for leaving Chrzanow by a day. This morning the horse-drawn wagons arrived in front of our apartment house, and we all started carrying stuff down the stairs to the sidewalk. Now Father is loading it onto the wagons, making sure to fill every inch of space. We are taking everything we might possibly use because we cannot afford the skyrocketing cost of replacements in Sosnowiec. As soon as the passenger wagon arrives we will be on our way.

The trip to Sosnowiec takes us through Jaworzno on Jagielonska Street, past our bus repair garage and the apartment house where Uncle Moses used to live. As we approach Mickiewicza Street, my curiosity gets the best of me and I want to get off the wagon and see our house again.

"Do you want to get us all arrested and shipped to Auschwitz?" Father demands. I cringe at his harsh tone and stay put.

We share the road with hundreds of other Jews – some on foot with large bundles on their shoulders, others in horse-drawn wagons. It is very sad to see our people being pushed around in this cruel way, and I cannot help but think, *why we did not pack up and leave Poland to go to Palestine at the time our grandfather left? Everyone was aware of Krystal Nacht and what was going on in Germany.* And then I remember what Father said: *Should have and would have does not help us now!*

As we approach the outskirts of Sosnowiec, I see rows of apartment houses four and five stories tall—all attached to one another and separated from the street by iron gates. My first thought is *if we live in one of these buildings, how can we hide or keep from being caught in a German raid?* Finally, we arrive at a four-story building and drive into the courtyard. Our apartment is on the third floor facing the yard.

My father decides to unload all our stuff onto the ground in order to avoid paying "waiting fees" for the wagons. My mother and Aunt Esther are to guard the luggage while Father and the rest of us carry whatever we can manage up the stairs to the apartment.

It has taken us a long time getting everything into the apartment; we finished just before dark. Now all of us are sitting on mattresses on the floor, sharing sandwiches that my mother and Aunt Esther prepared last night. We are all so exhausted, we won't even set up any of the beds or unpack any of the stuff. All we want to do is fall asleep on the floor.

It's a new day in more ways than one. As soon as I get done helping Father set up the bed frames and putting the mattresses on top of them, I go and check out the neighborhood, hoping to find out the best way to avoid being caught during raids.

Sosnowiec is totally unlike anything I have ever experienced, because everyone is so crowded together. Here, not only are the buildings all attached and the gates locked, there are no fields or bushes or trees where a person can hide. Again I think that this will make it very easy for the Germans to capture us Jews during raids.

Now I know more about my new home. Sosnowiec is a city served by cable cars and buses going all the way to the suburbs, but Jews are not allowed to travel on them. In the city, groceries and vegetables are limited and overpriced, so in order to get fresh produce, a person has to go to the Christian suburbs.

This, of course, creates many hardships for Jews, but it also lets me dress up like a Christian boy and start trading again. My parents don't like it, but they have no choice. They have no way to make a living, and we have to eat.

This will not be easy. It will take me awhile to learn cable car routes and find reliable sources of food at competitive prices. If I get caught, I will be shipped to Auschwitz. That scares me, but I don't dare show it. I also worry that I look too Jewish. I have very curly hair, which is a dead giveaway.

Now I've learned the cable car routes and started going to the suburbs to trade, but it's very dangerous. Many times, my heart pounds so hard I'm sure the other passengers can hear it. For one thing, they give me hostile stares. I'm sure they get suspicious when they see me carrying large bundles. Yet it's amazing how I can tune in to my surroundings and instantly detect dangers. This ability has helped me avoid many close scrapes with the law.

My Cousin and I
Are Caught in a Raid

Today, something awful happened. While I was walking my cousin Janek from one of his classes, we were caught in a German raid and taken to a prison called the *Dulag,* which is on a side street near the Jewish quarter. Across the street is a three story gray building where children are usually taken. But this time the Germans have dumped us in with the men. They will keep us here until they have gathered enough people for a transport to the Auschwitz-Birkenau concentration camps.

The Germans allow us to take turns going out into the courtyard to get some fresh air. When my turn comes, I realize that the courtyard is surrounded by a tall wall with glass shards imbedded in the concrete. Against the wall are three wooden sheds. There is also a pile of wooden planks about three meters (yards) long and odd pieces of lumber filled with rusted nails. It occurs to me that if we attach the lumber with the rusty nails to a wooden plank, we might be able to hoist the plank on top of the wooden shed and lean it against the wall. Then we could use the plank as a ladder, lay a piece of lumber over the glass shards, climb up the plank, hoist ourselves over the top and jump to freedom. I try this idea out on a few of the adult prisoners, and they think it's worth a shot. So I climb up first and Janek follows me. But as I reach the top of the plank, I realize that I am not tall enough to reach the top of the wall, and Janek—who is smaller than I am—certainly wouldn't be able to make it. Oh, well, it seemed like a good idea and maybe it will help other prisoners escape.

The next time we're in the yard, I realize that Janek and I are small enough to slip into the shed, where there are some slits in the wall large enough to slip notes through to the other side. We have now written several notes and slipped them through the wall, hoping that someone will pick them up and deliver them to our family so they will know where we are.

We've now spent three nights in the adult prison, but this morning we were moved to the smaller building across the street. This building is full of children, and every hour brings more— including babies. With so many people gathered here, I'm terrified that we will be sent directly to the death camp.

All of these children, who were brutally torn from their mothers' arms, are constantly crying. There are no toilets, so they just go to the bathroom on the floor. The sound of wailing children and the stench around here are enough to drive me out of my mind. And now we aren't allowed to leave the building for a breath of fresh air. I feel like an animal trapped in a cage and, to make it worse, nobody has answered our notes.

Tonight at dinner the Nazis announced that we would all be taken to a special youth camp tomorrow morning. I told Janek that this is one big lie—we must run for our lives the first chance we get, even if it means jumping off a transport truck while it is in motion.

This morning the Germans fed us cereal and told us, "In an hour you will be taken to a place where you will have many playgrounds and schools with wonderful teachers." I turned to Janek and told him again not to believe a word. I asked him to promise me that he would follow me when I made an escape.

Through the wrought iron bars that cover the windows of this room, I can see German military trucks pull up in front of the building. They are covered with green canvas tarps. Pacing around the trucks are SS guards with machine guns slung over their shoulders.

As we are told to line up two-by-two at the top of the stairs leading to the door where the trucks are waiting, I am amazed to see how obedient the children are.

Now the doors are opening and the line has started moving. Outside I can see the children climbing into one of the trucks. Suddenly the line stops, and the SS guards remove the steps and slam the rear gate of the truck shut. The engine starts and the truck leaves.

Immediately, another truck pulls up. The SS guards open the rear gate and pull the step ladder up, ready for the next batch of victims. Judging by the number of children ahead of us, I figure that we are going to be on this truck. My heart is racing a mile a minute because I don't have any idea what to do.

I turn to Janek and say, "We must escape before we get onto this truck." I turn to the kids in front of us and tell them that we are all going to get killed–that they will never see their parents again. I tell them that the whole story of a children's camp and playground is a big fat lie, and I ask them to start crying and yelling.

The line is moving again. Now we are going down a few steps and onto the sidewalk. Suddenly I realize that we are about 50 yards from a street with residential buildings. I figure this is our only chance to make a quick dash and try to reach safety. But we're still being pushed along– right up to the truck. Janek is ahead of me, and he's already climbing the ladder with me right behind him.

Suddenly the kids at the bottom of the ladder start screaming. As the SS guards turn to them, I quickly pulled Janek by the sleeve and yell in Polish "*Uciekamy*" (Let's run for it).

Now I'm running towards the intersection as fast as I can. I know that Janek is somewhere behind me, but I don't dare turn around. This is our only chance.

Around the corner and across the street is an apartment building where we can hide. I turn the corner, knowing that the German guards can't see me anymore. But when I get to the building, the gate is locked! I run to the next building and try that gate, but it, too, is locked. All I can think to do is open the lid of a large garbage bin in front of the building and climb in. I can't take any chances, so I take the garbage from the bottom of the bin and cover my body.

Suddenly I can hear the voices of the SS all around me. My heart is beating so wildly, I'm afraid that the whole garbage bin is shaking. But as I listen, the voices begin moving away, and this buys me a little more time.

Now I start worrying about Janek. What will I say when my parents want to know what happened to him? Janek doesn't even know where I am.

I don't know how long I've been here, but outside it's been quiet for a while. Now I can hear voices nearby speaking Polish, so I guess it's okay to lift the lid of the garbage bin and see what's going on.

The street seems to be calm. As far as I can see, there are no German police in the area, so I think it's safe to climb out of my hiding place.

I try to shake the garbage off my clothing and melt into the crowd. I wish I didn't smell so bad, but I finally get up enough courage to ask a young couple for directions.

I tell them who I am and what has happened, and I ask them to lend me fifty *groszy* for the cable car. They give me the change and tell me to keep it. They also tell me that the SS had a shortage of people to fill their transport, so they raided the neighboring houses. That certainly explains why I couldn't get into any of the buildings.

Now, though, I enter into the courtyard of a building with a fountain, and before getting on the cable car I wash my face and hands, trying to get rid of the odor of garbage that clings to me. *Oh, God*, I think, *what am I going to tell Aunt Esther about Janek? I don't know where he is or what has happened to him.*

I get off the cable car around the corner from where we live and walk slowly to our building, not knowing what to expect. When I get to our apartment, I put my ear to the door trying to hear what is going on inside. But all I can hear is my little brother Benek and my cousin Shlomek playing and laughing.

I slowly open the door, and as I walk in Shlomek and Benek start shouting, "Shmilek is here! Shmilek is here!" In the next room the entire family is sitting with Janek and listening to his story of the escape.

I am so excited to see Janek. We all hug each other, and now it's my turn to tell the story of *my* escape.

Another Forced Move— to Shrodula Ghetto

It's taken me a few days to get over the ordeal I went through last week, and I find that I have mixed feelings about it. Of course I'm glad that I can act decisively and with courage when I have to. And I'm proud that I was able to help Janek—and maybe other people—escape from the *Dulag*. But the fact that I felt it was my fault we were captured bothers me a great deal. It has taught me not to be so cocky in the future, to exercise greater caution.

The most important lesson I learned, though, is that **I never want to just wait for the Nazis to take me.** As a matter of fact, it makes me sick to see how most Jews just sit and wait to be taken.

Sometimes I wish I were old enough to join the resistance fighters in the forest and fight the Nazis. Other times I wish I were in Palestine working to end the problem of Jewish persecution, which our people have suffered for centuries.

If our family had gone there, we would not have been in this terrible mess to start with! But life for us is what it is, and I have a duty to bring in money and help the family survive these most difficult times.

While I'm thinking these thoughts, the Germans come up with new orders of resettlement or deportation. This time they have said that the Jewish population of Sosnowiec must relocate to a ghetto called Shrodula, about half a mile from the city's last cable car stop.

We've moved and now we're more crowded than ever. In addition to Aunt Esther we now live with Uncle Moses and his wife and daughters, Ruzia and Malusia, his brothers-in-law, Sam and David Klapholtz, and Uncle Israel. Fifteen of us now live on the bottom floor of a building, one floor below street level.

To enter the apartment from the street level, you have to go down a flight of concrete steps into the yard. This would normally be considered a basement apartment, but the building is on an incline that gives us a clear view of the valley below, all the way to the last

Srodula Ghetto, where I lived in a basement with 14 other people

cable car stop. The fields in between are covered with weeds and overgrown bushes.

It is quite clear to us that the reason for moving the Jews into this fenced ghetto is to make it easier for the Nazis to conduct their raids.

The ghetto is governed by a *Judenrat*, which is a board of Jewish elders. They picked the police force and armed them with night sticks, but they have no real authority. They just carry out the Germans' orders.

No one is allowed to leave the ghetto without a valid pass issued by the *Judenrat* and stamped by the police. This has turned out to be a source of income for the *Judenrat* and police, and now passes are sold on the black market to the highest bidder.

To avoid the ridiculous fees for passes, my Uncle Israel came up with a good idea. He climbed over the wall of our yard to find the thickest bushes that grow next to the wall. Inside the courtyard, my father was waiting beside the wall with a hammer and chisel. When

Uncle Israel found a spot on the wall that was covered by a dense growth of leafy bushes, he tapped on the wall so that Father could start to chisel out an opening that would be hidden from view on the outside. Once Father broke through the wall, he handed Uncle Israel another hammer and chisel so that they could complete the job faster.

Once that job was finished, Uncle Israel slid into the yard through the hole to make sure that it could be done. Then he and Father took a rusty old tool cabinet and placed it on the inside of the wall to cover the opening. This hole has been a life saver, because I can use it every day when I go out to trade—without having to pay for passes.

Within our ghetto, the black market is the only game in town. Jankel, the shoemaker, needs leather to fix soles on his customers' shoes. Simon, the tailor, needs cloth to make suits and dresses. Mothers need milk and cereal for their babies. Folks *outside* the ghetto need the things we produce *in* the ghetto. This need has created a lively trade between the two communities.

So now I get up at dawn and slip through the hole in our wall, dressed as a Polish student. One day I might carry a bag full of pants and shoes, which I sell on the black market outside. From the proceeds of the sale, I buy all sorts of food and whiskey to bring back to the black market in the ghetto. And so it goes. But it's dangerous. The German police and the SS never come into the ghetto except when they conduct raids, which they now do more and more often.

In Jewish tradition, at age 13 a boy makes the transition from boyhood to manhood, which is a cause for a celebration called the *Bar Mitzvah*. My *Bar Mitzvah* is only a month away—August 1942—and I have not even had a chance to study for it. Our family's need for money has come first. And so I have been busy trading and smuggling from dawn to dusk. My father has been helping me at night to memorize a portion of the Torah (the five books of Moses), which I will have to read during a Monday morning prayer session.

My *Bar Mitzvah* has passed and was celebrated without too much fanfare. I was met and congratulated by the entire family when we returned from the service and that was pretty much it. But today, from our vantage point looking out over the fields, we noticed a convoy of German military vehicles heading towards us. We knew that they were going to conduct a raid in the streets of the ghetto, so we quickly locked our doors and stayed in the house until the raid was over. This time, though, the Germans entered apartments at random to catch as many people as they could—just to fill their transports to the concentration camps.

This development poses an enormous problem for us, and right now we're not sure how to solve it. Uncle Moses, who has many contacts outside the ghetto, has offered to get in touch with a lady named Pani Cichowa, who lives on the outskirts of Sosnowiec and once offered to hide a certain number of Jews in her basement.

We have decided that Aunt Sarah, who doesn't look Jewish, little three-year-old Malusia and Uncle Israel should hide there. If things work out well, other members of the family might be able to join them later.

In the meantime, in order to protect the rest of the family from being caught in the raids, we should seal off a section of our apartment with brick walls that have a hidden entrance. My father, who did such a great job of hiding our family treasures in the walls in Jaworzno, will be in charge of the project.

Father has walled in an entire section of the apartment with a brick wall. He has left a three-foot by three-foot opening for a hidden entrance and has built wooden bunks on three walls of the hideout. He even built a kitchen stove with an oven up against the wall of the opening. We will use the hinged door of the oven to slide into and out of the hideout. We've had a few practice runs to make sure we can get in and out quickly.

Everything has gone like clockwork. No one looking at the stove against the wall would ever suspect that it is a fake. I am very proud of my contribution to the project. I bought most of the building materials for the stove on the black market outside the ghetto. They were very heavy and I had to make many dangerous trips.

Lately, the German police have increased their foot patrols along the outside of the ghetto to stop our smuggling. One day I was spotted by a German policeman as I was carrying a bag full of food and whiskey to be sold in the ghetto. All of a sudden I heard him yelling at me, "Halt! Halt!"

Instead of stopping, I started running as fast as I could towards the wall of the ghetto. While I was running, I pulled out a bottle of brandy from the bag and dropped it gently onto the path. Sure enough, he stopped to pick it up, and while he was busy checking out the contents of the bottle I was able to run to the dense bushes that grew along the wall and slide into our yard. It turned out that some of my relatives were watching the whole thing, and they later congratulated me for distracting the policeman. I was extremely lucky that it worked out the way it did, but by now I have had so many brushes with the Nazis that I am quick to react to any threatening situation.

The Fateful Day Arrives

It's now early in the Spring of 1943, and conditions in the ghetto have become unbearable. People have no way to make a living, and many are starving. The Nazis conduct raids every week and ship people off to the labor camps in Germany and the Auschwitz and Birkenau extermination camps near here.

Through it all, our people are meek and submissive, and that infuriates me. I guess that being persecuted for 2,000 years has sapped the heroic blood from their veins. But here's what I think: knowing full well that we are going to be killed, why not take a few Nazis with us to the grave?

Conditions at home have taken a bad turn. My sister Rachel was taken to the hospital with a badly infected leg. Now the doctors say she has gangrene, and there are no medications to treat it. Her leg will have to be amputated.

When they learned this, my parents told Benek and me that Rachel would be an invalid for the rest of her life. They asked us to promise that whatever happens to her in the future, we will stand by her side and help her to live a dignified life. Of course we agreed.

I feel so bad that I cannot tear myself away from my responsibilities to visit her in the hospital, but to tell the truth I don't want to see her in a helpless condition. She has always been so full of life and wisdom, it would be heartbreaking.

On August 1, 1943 the thing we have dreaded comes to pass. Two long columns of German military vehicles have lined up in front of the entrance gate to our ghetto, and soldiers with machine guns have taken up positions all along the outside wall. We know that there is no escape.

Even so, we run down the stairs and head for our hiding place, which we call "the Bunker." Everyone, including some neighbors, slides through the "oven" door. All together, there are 24 people, including some babies.

In this hidden room there is no ventilation. The only air we have comes through a three-inch pipe that passes from the chimney through the bunker walls. We have enough emergency food and water here to last 14 people for 24 hours. Now, it will have to stretch to take care of 10 more.

After we sit in silence for some time, we hear the roaring sound of heavy trucks passing in the street and feel the vibration they make. Soon afterwards, we can hear loudspeakers announcing the liquidation of the ghetto. The voice asks all residents to assemble in the public square with all the belongings they can carry.

We have no way of knowing what exactly is happening outside, but suddenly we hear pounding and knocking, followed by heavy footsteps, in the apartment above us. We can clearly hear the Germans ordering people to go to the public square.

Now, we hear a German soldier's boots moving to the exit door, and for a moment we think we are safe. But all of a sudden one of the babies starts to cry, and its panic-stricken mother quickly covers the baby's head with a pillow so its crying will not reveal our hiding place to the Germans.

After about five minutes the Germans come back to the apartment above us and start chopping the wooden floor with their axes. As pieces of wood and splinters come raining down on us, she removes the pillow from her baby's face. To our horror, the child is dead.

"Oh my God, I smothered my baby to death! I'm sorry! I'm sorry! I caused the bunker to be exposed!" she wails.

We try to pacify her by saying that the Germans have dogs with them and would have detected us anyway, but nothing we say comforts her.

The Nazis shout at us, ordering us to join the rest of the ghetto residents in the public square. There is nothing we can do now but climb up through the broken floor to the apartment above us and go out onto the sidewalk.

My parents, Benek and the rest of the family go downstairs to gather all the belongings we may need and are able to carry. Then all 14 of us, with bags of clothing on our shoulders, drag ourselves up the stairs and onto the sidewalk.

Ahead of us the old and the feeble, children and couples with babies in their arms walk in one long line that looks like a funeral procession. *What they don't know,* I think, *is that they are marching to their own funerals.*

As we move reluctantly to the public square, Mother suddenly wonders what will happen to our sister Rachel. The rest of us know that the Nazis will drag all the patients from the hospital straight into the gas chambers at Auschwitz-Birkenau, but we say nothing.

Now we are surrounded on all sides by Nazis, and there is no possibility of escape. The voice on the loudspeakers keeps blaring out the same message: everyone must move into the public square. It is driving me crazy. And the worst thing is, we don't know what's going to happen. All we can hear is the hysterical cries of women and children.

All the while, uniformed SS officers, with trained dogs at their sides, are directing us into the square, which is sectioned off by ropes. SS guards stand at the entrance to each section.

Now we are being directed to a long line that, it turns out, is waiting to pass through the "selection station." As the line inches forward, I can see how the selection process works and suddenly I realize why the cries of the women and children were so heart wrenching. The Germans are tearing babies off their mothers' breasts and throwing them on the ground. They are separating women from their families. It is a hellish scene that words can't even begin to describe.

As the line moves ahead, I can clearly see that there is one section with only women and children, another with old people and invalids and yet another with healthy looking young men and women. There is also a roped-off section that looks like an empty lot. I wonder what this is for.

As Father sees what is taking place, he decides that the family should split up. He tells me I should try to stay with him and says Benek should stay with Mother. We all know that once we are separated, we may never see one another again.

The tears stream down our cheeks as we hug and kiss and wish one another the best. All around us, we hear the agonizing cries of all the families that are being torn apart.

I can see that the Germans have the liquidation of this ghetto of 35,000 Jews planned down to the last detail. At the end of each roped-off section, a line of trucks is waiting to haul us off to Auschwitz. In the front and rear of each truck, German Wehrmacht (regular army) soldiers are making sure that people get loaded onto the trucks quickly.

The Germans are going to liquidate 35,000 people without a single shot being fired at them. How can we let this happen? What makes Jews so meek and willing to endure humiliation, extermination, and persecution—to consider it "the will of God?" This is what I'm thinking as I wait to learn if I will live or die.

But now another thing occurs to me. I start worrying that I won't end up in the same group as my father because I am so young and small. The next time the Nazi guard isn't looking, I'm going to move far enough back from my father to see which section he's being sent to. Then when the SS guard turns his back again, I'll quickly run to join that group.

44

Father has been directed to take his place in a group of fit men between the ages of 18 and 50. They are lining up in five long rows. Now I have to wait for a chance to make a run for it.

In front of me is a couple with two children. The SS man is separating the husband from his wife and two children, directing him to join the same group my father is in. As he moves away, one of his kids starts crying and running after him. Roughly, the SS man grabs the child and takes him back to his mother.

Now's my chance. While his back is turned, I'll make a quick dash to join my father's group.

So far so good, but as I reach the rear of the group, I suddenly realize that I'm the smallest and youngest one there. Unless I come up with some inventive idea, they will send me back to the children's section, which is headed straight for the gas chambers. I need something to stand on that will make me look taller.

I'm in luck! Near the wall of the ghetto, I find half of a concrete block, which I place on the ground at the end of my fathers' row. As I get up on it, I find that now I'm the same height as the others.

When the SS comes around to question the men about their occupations, they start with the front row. I hear them ask my father, *"Haben sie ein beruf?"* (Do you have an occupation?)

"Ja ich bin ein maurer" (Yes, I am a mason), my father replies.

He is told to go to the group on the left, where the able-bodied and young men are.

When the German turns to me, I look straight into his monocle as he asks, *"Was machst du den? "* (What are you doing?)

"Ich bin ein maurers helfer" (I am a mason's assistant) I answer, and he orders me to go to the same group as my father. I wait a few seconds to make sure he does not see me stepping off the concrete block, and with a huge sigh of relief I join my father's group.

I can't tell you how elated I am to be with my father. I love and respect him very much and want to be with him. But I have to make sure not to cling to him because that would hurt his chances for survival.

We are safe for now. We will be taken to a work camp and not the gas chamber. While I was trying to save my own skin, I didn't hear the sobbing and screaming of mothers being separated from their loved ones. I didn't hear the babies crying when they were torn from their mothers' arms. And now I can't help but wonder if *God* hears all these cries? If He does, why doesn't He do something to help these people? Does God have something else on His agenda that is so important He has to ignore all this pain and suffering?

I fail to understand why Jewish people go to their deaths with these words on their lips: *Shma Israel Adonai Eloheinu Adonai Echad* (Hear, O Israel, God is our God, there is only one God). What kind of way of paying tribute to God is this? I have had this discussion with my father—expressed my rage to him about this kind of martyrdom—but it has gotten me nowhere and has always left me fuming. His answer always is, "We cannot question God's' plan."

Once I told my father, " If I am always left to my own devices and cannot expect God to help me, why should I believe in God?" Father's answer was, "Belief in God must not be questioned. It is our tradition!"

Now, all around me I see people violating the moral values that have always been at the heart of Jewish teaching and tradition. Look at the *Judenrat*—the Jewish elders who help the Nazis just so that they might save their own skins. And what about the Jewish police who enforced the Germans' rules on their fellow Jews as they did during the liquidation of the Shrodula ghetto? Even the Nazis have no respect for these people.

Once, this even happened in my own family. The brother-in-law of my Uncle Moses, Samuel Klapholtz, traveled with Nazi officers to various labor camps in Germany, where he met with the inmates and gained their confidence. They would tell him where their families' jewels and valuables were buried in exchange for promises of better food rations and special privileges. But none of his promises were kept.

He simply helped the Nazis rob his fellow Jews and took some of the loot for himself.

Once I had a confrontation with him and called him a *musor* (traitor), for which he slapped me in the face. Even my father had some harsh words for him in my defense.

Even now, the Jewish police are doing the bidding of the Nazis. A Jewish policeman has ordered us to put all our belongings in one pile and line up to get on the trucks that will take us to our new destination. He told us that our belongings will be put on a separate truck and we will get them back. A likely story!

As I'm having these black thoughts, our line is moving in an orderly fashion. Clearly, there's no way for me to escape. Even if I had a place to escape *to,* the Nazis would soon find out from the Jewish police whose son I am. Then they would take Father out and shoot him in front of the whole group as a warning: *this is what happens when someone tries to escape.*

Father and I Are Taken to Annaberg Labor Camp

Now we've reached the truck. As I climb up into it, I turn around to see if I can get a last glimpse of Mother and Benek and wave goodbye. But the square is so crowded I cannot see them. My eyes well up with tears.

On the truck I sit down on one of the two planks that are used as benches. My father is seated diagonally across from me.

Once the truck is fully loaded, the rear gate is pulled up and the tarp is lowered, leaving us in total darkness. The truck's engine roars to life and we inch out of the public square. As the agonizing sound of people's cries gradually fades, I can hear the revving of the SS motorcycles that are escorting our truck.

Here in the darkness of the truck, I am left with only the memory of my last glimpse of the public square — a picture of hell on earth, where babies are torn from their mothers' breasts, wives are separated from their husbands and children are taken from their fathers.

Suddenly my head seems to be spinning like a merry-go-round as I see, in my mind's eye, all the members of my large family and wonder what has happened to them. As I see my sister Rachel in her hospital bed and wonder what her fate will be. When the merry-go-round stops spinning, I open my eyes and wonder if the people sitting next to me feel the same pain and anguish I do. I'll bet every person on this truck has a suitcase full of sorrows that he will carry with him all of his life. What a pitiful world!

After a two-hour journey the truck comes to a halt at our labor camp, Annaberg. The tarps are raised, the gate is lowered and we are ordered to get off the truck and assemble in an open field for registration and assignment to living quarters. It's still daylight, so I can take a good look at the surrounding area. The camp is in a deep forest, and a strong fragrance from the pine trees fills the air. The camp is completely enclosed by a barbed wire fence, with watchtowers spaced about 50 meters (yards) apart for as far as the eye can see.

Now the entire transport of prisoners is lined up in rows of five people deep, ready to be processed. While waiting for the roll call, I look around to check out the surrounding area and see if there is any possible way for us to escape. It doesn't look promising: the barbed-wire fence and sentry towers make an escape unlikely, and there are several white signs with a red skeleton head and the words *Achtung Hochspannung,* (Warning High Tension) painted on them. Clearly this means that the fence is electrified and anyone attempting to escape will be electrocuted.

I have some other major concerns, too. For one thing, I could not consider escaping without my father. They would torture and then execute him if they found out that I had escaped. And then there's the dense forest, where an escaped prisoner could get lost or be attacked by wild animals.

Needless to say, I don't plan to share my thoughts of escape with my father–he would tell me that I'm going nuts. But I can't stop

An electric fence and barbed wire discourage thoughts of escape.

thinking about escape. It's my nature to try to find my way out when I feel trapped.

We've been standing here a long time without knowing what we're waiting for, but now a group of SS troopers with large German shepherds on leashes is coming towards us. Behind them is a group of men in blue and white striped uniforms with caps on their heads.

"These men are fellow prisoners," the SS commander bellows through his bullhorn. "They've come here to help you. They are responsible for making sure that all our orders are faithfully carried out."

These men are Jews who are known as *capos*, and they will have control of our daily lives. They do this in exchange for extra food, real mattresses and other privileges for themselves. Pathetic!

"Our" *capo* tells us that we must be thoroughly clean before we can be assigned to our barracks. He orders us to undress and give him all our valuables. Then he takes us to a line of barbers, who shave our heads. As if this weren't insulting enough, our bodies are sprayed with the disinfectant Lysol. I thought that was only used to clean toilets, but now it's used to clean *us*!

Before we enter the showers, we are handed a bar of soap that feels like it's made of sand and a towel made of linen that can't soak up water. When we come out of the shower, *capos* with night sticks rush at us and herd us to an assembly point for another roll call. We grab whatever we can, but we must keep moving to avoid being clubbed by the *capos*.

In the process we discover that while we were in the showers, our clothing was gone through with a fine-tooth comb. Father lost a treasured pocket watch that had been in his family for generations and Swiss bank notes that were sewn into the collar of his jacket.

At roll call in the *Appellplatz* (assembly place), we are each given a patch with a number, which we are to sew onto the left side of our shirt. From now on, we will only be identified by that number—as if we are no longer human beings with names. My father has been given *heftlings nummer 178508* (prisoner number 178508) and I am 178509. The *capos* know that we are related.

Next, we are divided into work groups and assigned to rooms in the barracks. In each barrack, there are eight rooms with two rows of seven bunks. There are 28 prisoners to a room and 224 to a barrack. Between each pair of bunks in our room are four cubbyholes with hinged doors where we are to keep our personal items and the food rations they give us. I will share a bunk bed with my father, with him on the bottom and me on the top.

In the middle of the barrack is a narrow hall with a washroom on one side and a bathroom on the other. The bathroom has no stalls—just open rows of toilets—and there are two long funnels instead of sinks. Above each funnel, there are no faucets, just a pipe with holes punched in it.

By now we are all starving, so we are glad when someone from the kitchen finally arrives with a bucket of hot soup. A *capo* ladles some out to each of us, but it's watery and disgusting. Each of us also gets a daily ration of bread and margarine, but when I finish eating I am still hungry. If this is all the food we'll get, I can't imagine how it will be enough to keep us going through days of hard work. But there's one hope: each week we prisoners will each get a ration of *machorka*, a coarse tobacco that is made of wood pulp and sugar. Since Father and I don't smoke, we may be able to trade our tobacco rations for four-ounce sugar rations, and that would be an enormous help in maintaining the strength we need for our hard work.

Before he leaves, the *capo* tells us that our wake-up call comes at 7:00 a.m. and we must all be lined up at the assembly place at 7:30 to receive our work orders.

Sure enough, at exactly 7:00 a.m. the sirens go off, and *capos* with bullhorns are in our barrack rushing us to go to the *Appellplatz* for roll call. This results in a stampede to the toilets and washroom, which is actually very dangerous because people are almost trampled to death as they try to avoid being beaten by the *capos*. Nevertheless, Father and I make it to roll call in one piece.

At roll call, Father is told he'll be sent to work on construction of new barracks in the freshly excavated areas of the camp and I am to be his assistant. First, we are to dig trenches for the foundation and set up the forms with steel re-enforcing rods. Then before we can pour the foundation, we have to wait for an inspection by a Nazi engineer. The Nazis won't allow us to use cement mixers, so we must mix everything by hand.

While the freshly poured cement is curing, the Nazis make us dig trenches to prepare for the next foundation. All this time, the *capos* are standing over us with sticks in their hands, making sure that we never stop working.

During the lunch break, the kitchen detail, under the supervision of a *capo*, comes to dole out more of their watery soup to us. We quickly find out that most of the prisoners want to be last in the soup line so

At 7 a.m. each day we are forced to line up in the Appellplatz. This photo was taken at another camp, Buchenwald, in Germany. (United States Holocaust Memorial Museum American Jewish Joint Distribution Committee, Yad Vashem Photo Archives, courtesy of Robert A. Schmuhl)

52

that they can get a few morsels of vegetable from the bottom of the bucket. This leads to much arguing and shoving and even fights. No matter—our *capo* usually saves the best ingredients for his favorite prisoners.

The problem as I see it is that this does not result in immediate starvation. These poor people just linger on as they gradually turn from human beings into skeletons that suffer an agonizing death. The Germans exploit us until our last breath to perform manual labor for them.

Because Annaberg is an isolated camp located in a forest and all our work is performed inside the camp, we usually have no contact with the outside world. However, once in a while men who are not German bring construction materials into camp, and then we find out what is happening in the rest of Europe. One day we found out that the Russians broke through the German lines and are advancing westward towards Germany. We also heard that the Allies landed in France.

News like this is a morale booster for us, even though it doesn't lessen our misery. The drudgery of doing the same hard work on a starvation diet every single day is very hard for me to take. Oh, I don't mind what the hard labor and starvation diet do to my body; it's the mental and emotional anguish of being trapped in a cage with no hope of escape that drives me crazy.

Some nights I wake up in a fit of anger, as I try to dream and scheme my way out of this miserable confinement. But in the morning, I get up to face the same boring routine. I'm used to being able to scheme my way out of almost any uncomfortable situation, but here all I can do is complain about it.

Fortunately my father is always around to lend me an ear and allow me to blow off steam. I don't know what I would do without him. He's like a saint who is able to calm me down by constantly preaching the importance of faith and optimism. He keeps insisting that with "patience, optimism, hope and perseverance" we will survive this ordeal. He used to add *faith* to that list, but he knows how irritated I get with that word. I always tell him, "Faith is blind. A person cannot face the world with closed eyes and a closed mind."

We surely have our differences, but I love him for it. Only *he* is able to pound some sense into my head and get me to be practical about our situation, because any action on my part would result in tragedy.

The construction project we are assigned to is nearly finished. Each crew, from the foundation guys to the finished roof guys, had its tasks well defined and organized. The Nazis are good at that.

Of course the *capos* have made sure to claim credit, and now they are looking to get their reward. The Nazis have given them free reign to do with the prisoners as they wish. I've heard it said that power corrupts, and the *capos* use their power whenever they can to win favor with their Nazi masters. They beat prisoners whenever they fail to meet a production quota or a scheduled completion date. They even deny daily food rations to those who do not comply with their whims. This is very cruel punishment because the prisoners who are denied their rations often get sick. And no prisoner is allowed to be sick for more than two days. Otherwise, he will be sent to the medical section, where he will be given a lethal injection. Then his corpse will be sent to the crematorium.

All I can say is, "When you live in hell, you get used to the heat." I guess it's a hell of a way to live.

Our Next Hell Hole—
Blechhammer

Today we completed our project. Now, back in the barracks area, the alarms suddenly go off and the *capos* run around with their bullhorns ordering everyone to report for roll call at the *Appellplatz*. We are given orders to be there at 7:00 the following morning.

At 6:00 a.m. the sirens go off and the *capos* go from barrack to barrack with their bullhorns, bellowing, "All prisoners must take all their belongings, including their tin canisters and blankets, to roll call." Strange.

Once outside, I see a row of trucks at the camp gate and I know something is up. It doesn't take long to find out *what.* After we assemble, we are told to line up and move towards the trucks.

By now I'm used to the process, except that this time the trucks have no planks to sit on—standing room only! Within minutes, the gate is closed, the tarps are pulled down, the motorcycles begin to rev and we are on our way. We're packed in so tight, it shouldn't be hard to stand up, but the truck is rocking so violently it *is* hard. Luckily, the trip only lasts a half hour. As the truck slows and comes to a stop, we hear music. The gate is lowered and the tarp is pulled up by men in blue and white uniforms. As we get off the truck. I see a barbed wire fence with double gates. Next to the gates, on a wooden platform, a group of musicians is playing tunes from various nations. The musicians are also dressed in blue and white uniforms. I think *this is very nice of them to welcome us with live music. Maybe life will be better here.*

As we march towards the *Appellplatz,* I notice many similarities between this place and Annaberg. For one thing, Blechhammer is located in the midst of a very dense forest. It, too, has a double barbed wire fence with watchtowers every 50 meters. The fence is totally electrified with the same white and red signs on the ground. Everything is almost a replica of Annaberg except for the size.

Blechhammer is much larger than Annaberg. Oh, and there is one other noticeable difference: on the ground between the two fences is wire mesh with spikes spread all over it.

This puzzles me, and I ask my father if he knows the significance of the wire mesh. He tells me that in addition to the fence being electrified, the Germans have put a minefield between the fences–just in case someone tries to escape during a power failure. He warns me not to even *think* about this as an escape route because it is certain suicide.

The remains of the concentration camp entrance and a watch tower. By 2000, when I took this photo, the forest had begun to reclaim this awful place.

The SS guards with their German shepherds, along with a group of *capos*, divide our transport into different work groups and assign us to barracks. I am again lucky to be assigned to the same room as my father.

That's the good news. The bad news is I am assigned to a different work group. In the morning, we are to line up with our work group, not with our barrack group.

Right now we are not allowed to go into our rooms until we pass through our delousing process (you know, the one that gets rid of any lice we may have picked up at our last camp).

First we have to take off all our clothes and go through a line to be examined by a doctor for various diseases. Then comes the dreaded haircut.

Here, the hair "styles" are somewhat different. In addition to cutting our hair short, the barbers make an even shorter path down the middle of our heads. They call it *Die Lause Strasse* (The Street for Lice). It would be funny if it weren't so insulting. And to top it all off, we are issued the same gritty soap.

After being doused with a layer of Lysol all over our bodies, we go into a room where a *capo* tells us that in this camp everyone wears a blue and white striped uniform. He hands one to each of us and gives us each a patch with our number on it. The patches will be sewn onto our jackets by a group of tailors. Then we are issued new tin canisters and striped bags for our rations.

Every work group has its own *capo* "commander." We are told exactly where to report to him for the 7:00 o'clock roll call the next morning.

Then we line up for our daily ration of bread and margarine and—you guessed it—watery soup. The weekly ration of sugar and tobacco will be issued on Saturday.

The barracks here are exactly like those at Annaberg, and Father and I will maintain the same sleeping arrangements we had there. As I get into my bunk, I wonder what it is going to be like the next morning, when I won't be going to work with my father.

Three-tiered concentration camp bunks

It is 6:00 a.m. sharp, and I am awakened by the shrill blare of sirens. Father is already standing at the side of the bunk saying his morning prayers. I give him a quick look and jump off my bunk to go to the latrine. There, the place is a madhouse. No toilet is available, and there's no spot at the water funnel where I can wash my face. Everybody is pushing and shoving, trying to get to the *Appellplatz* in time for roll call. No one wants to antagonize the *capo* at the first meeting.

When I go to get dressed, I have a problem with the blue and white uniform they gave me. It is *much* too big! I guess they didn't make the uniforms with a 14-year-old boy in mind. It takes me quite a while to fold up the bottom of my pants and the sleeves of my jacket so I look halfway decent. When I've done the best I can, I hug my father and we say goodbye as we leave the barrack to join our different work groups at the *Appellplatz*.

As I join my group, I begin to get quite scared because I don't know what to expect. But much to my surprise, my fellow prisoners give me a warm welcome. Even the *capo* asks me, "How the hell did *you* get in here?" I answer him, "I walked." He begins to laugh and says, "You are a wise guy, eh?" I decide I'd better leave it at that. It's not good to draw too much attention to myself. Nevertheless, I feel good that I broke the ice with a *capo*.

Now we line up in long rows, five men deep. The prisoners in the two outside rows are shackled, while the prisoners in the inside rows are handcuffed to each other. This makes escape impossible.

Our *capo* takes a head count of his work group and reports it to the SS camp commander. Then we start marching towards the exit gates. As we get close to the gates, I hear music and see the same musicians as yesterday on their wooden platform. Part of me thinks, *This is strange,* and part of me thinks, *I guess this is meant to cheer us up on the way to work.* If this is the case, I can't say it's working with me. Being shackled and handcuffed is terrifying, but I'm afraid to say anything to the men on either side of me. I figure they're probably terrified too. Besides, in addition to the *capo* who is leading our march, we are surrounded by SS guards, who march beside us.

When we first begin to move, we have to concentrate on coordinating our steps, but after awhile we get the idea and manage to avoid bumping into one another. It's a good thing because we have a long walk on a paved road that leads deep into the forest.

After what seems like an hour in the forest, suddenly we can see the sky and the chimneys of some industrial buildings on the horizon. This industrial complex is the *Baustelle,* (*bough-SCHTEL-uh*), which means "working complex." The area is protected by a nine-foot steel mesh fence and a rollaway gate.

Once we are inside the gate, we are led to a vast construction site, our shackles and handcuffs are taken off and we are assigned to different workstations. The *capo* assigns me to a small group and introduces me to a German welder named Herr (Mr.) Frank. I am told that I will be working as his helper, and I am to faithfully obey all his instructions and pay close attention to all his advice.

Herr Frank is a stocky man with dark hair and brown eyes. I immediately notice that he is wearing an old German *Wehrmacht* hat with earflaps. The *Wehrmacht* is made up mostly of men who have been forced into service and don't necessarily want to be working for Adolph Hitler and his Third Reich at all. I know that the Germans put all men between the ages of 18 and 50 into their armed forces. They are fighting on at least three fronts. In the East there is the Russian front. In the West there are the allied forces of the United States, Britain and France. And in Africa, there are the British. The need to send fighters

59

to all these fronts has created an enormous shortage of manpower, so the Nazis have had to draft all kinds of unwilling men and women.

All the time the *capo* is lecturing me, Herr Frank has a little smile on his face. When the *capo* leaves, he says, *"Du darfst kein angst haben, du darfst uberhaupt die sache nicht complicieren, alles ist ganz einfach"* (You need not be afraid, you need not complicate matters, everything is quite simple.) These words are very welcome. Herr Frank also tells me that I will learn the secrets of electric welding as long as I pay careful attention to what he is doing. I am not to rush into doing anything without clearing it with him first. And I must never watch him weld without using a welder's mask. He explains that without a mask, the intensity of the arc is so strong I could lose my eyesight.

This introduction is a pleasant surprise because I am not used to being treated well by a German. In fact, it makes me a little suspicious, but I decide not to jump to any conclusions. I wish my father were here; he surely would be able to give me the right advice.

Now it's time for Herr Frank's lunch. He takes an hour, usually between 12:00 and 1:00, but I don't have to line up until 12:30 and I only get a half hour. Since I'm not supposed to do anything without Herr Frank's approval, I decide to use the half hour between 12:00 and 12:30 to look around the *Baustelle* and see who else is working here.

To my surprise, I find that there are people from many other countries–English and French and Russian prisoners of war housed in separate camps and guarded by the *Wehrmacht*. In fact, I learn that there are many young men and women from all over Nazi-occupied Europe who have been forced to come here and work for very low wages, under slave-labor conditions.

Now it's time to get back to the lunch line. How I hope that the soup will be better here. But it is not to be. When the *capo* comes from the kitchen, he doles out the same watery soup that was served in Annaberg. Unfortunately, this results in the same jockeying for position in hopes of getting served from the bottom of the kettle.

It's nearly time to quit work. I must say I'm confused by the experiences I've had today, and I can hardly wait to discuss them with my father. At 4:30 on the dot, we line up to be handcuffed and shackled for the return march to our camp. As we walk through the deep forest, I keep thinking about the difference between the two camps. In Annaberg we were literally walled in, but here in Blechhammer there is at least a chance for us to be in touch with civilization through other types of prisoners. Never mind the fact that we are forbidden to make contact with anyone from the outside—we will do it anyway!

Back at camp I finally get a chance to talk with my father and ask him how his day went. He tells me that he is working as a tinsmith and really likes what he is doing. Then he asks me how my day went and what happened at the *Baustelle*. I tell him everything about my introduction to Herr Frank and the fact that he wore an old *Wehrmacht* cap. I tell Father that this man is a welder who is going to teach me the trade. I also tell him that Herr Frank walks with a limp, and Father asks me why. I say that I didn't want to ask him because it might be a touchy subject. Father agrees that it would be a good idea to wait awhile.

Then Father says that in his unit, they were able to speak to some English prisoners of war (POWs) who have secretly listened to the British Broadcasting Corporation on a hidden radio. He tells me about the progress being made on all fronts by the Allied and Russian forces. He even gives me a brief geography lesson to show me the progress being made on each front. Father explains that under the Geneva Convention, the American, French and British POWs are entitled to receive mail and packages from their homeland through the Red Cross. That is why they are so much better off than we are. He says that the Germans are not letting the mail through out of the goodness of their hearts. No, the allies have many German prisoners of war and the Germans want them to be treated in accordance with the laws of the Geneva Convention, which means treated well.

Our conversation is interrupted by the sound of a bullhorn. It's time to line up for our evening food ration: more weak soup and the same pushing and shoving to be at the end of the line. Yet I notice that my father never does this. He always maintains a calm, dignified manner. This prompts me to ask him, "Why are you so passive? Why do you accept everything that happens?"

He turns to me in a very calm way and says, "You must learn to accept the things you cannot change. Once you do that, you can channel your energy to change the things that really matter to you."

It is important to bear in mind that my father is a very religious orthodox Jew. He faithfully practices his religion, even in the worst situations. Here in camp, he prays every morning and evening and tries to follow the laws of our people regarding the food that we may eat. In a place where we are fed thin soup and a little bread this is very difficult to do, but he tries.

Now I think about what he has said and I find that it makes a lot of sense *in theory*. But, I tell my father, the reality is quite different.

"Here at age 14 I am being shackled and handcuffed every day just to go to and from work. I am surviving on a starvation diet. I constantly see people who have gotten so thin that they look like skeletons and so sick that they can no longer work. I see them sent to the infirmary, where they are put to death.

"With this kind of reality, I think I have the right to be furious. What meaning is there to life when I must work for the Nazis as long as my strength lasts and wind up looking like a skeleton and dying?"

Father waits for me to calm down and then tells me, "We cannot win a physical encounter with the Nazis, not under these conditions. At the same time, we must never let them reduce us to their level. We are the people of the book (the Bible), and we were given a higher standard of morals and behavior to live up to. If we violate those standards, we will be beasts like the Nazis are and hand them a victory."

His argument makes a lot of sense. I would like to be as noble as he is, but we live in a place of cruelty and torture. Even though I admire my father for being able to maintain his high moral standards here, I can't possibly maintain those standards for myself. I can't accept the belief that it is God's will that we suffer, and I don't believe in turning the other cheek.

Nevertheless, I love my father for sticking to his principals. I especially like the idea of accepting the things I cannot change. In fact, I have tried very hard to put it into practice in my daily life because it gives me hope.

Unfortunately, following Father's advice is easier said than done. I still can't accept being shackled and handcuffed every day, knowing that it is something I cannot change. Before we were sent to Annaberg, I found many ways to help our family. I thrived on being creative and outsmarting the Germans. And that's the way I want to be now.

Today when I got to hear news of how the war is going, I *did* see a reason for us to hope that we may live to see freedom again. And Herr Frank gives me hope.

It's a new day, and I again realize how fortunate I am to have a German supervisor who is so lenient and understanding and treats me so well. Again, I wonder why he is so much different than the other Germans. And again I notice that he is limping. Finally I gather enough courage to ask him. His answer surprises me.

He tells me that one day he was drafted into the *Wehrmacht* and sent to the Russian front. There, he was injured during the battle of Stalingrad. Fortunately, he was sent to a military hospital in Germany, where he was treated for his wounds and given six months of physical therapy before being released into civilian life. Herr Frank also makes it clear that he is in total disagreement with the policies of the Nazi regime.

In spite of this conversation, I feel it is too soon for me to be able to trust him.

I guess I forgot to tell you that the concentration camp prisoners are treated much more harshly than the foreign nationals and prisoners of war here. We are not allowed to use the same toilets or take cover in a bomb shelter when Allied planes fly over the camp and the air raid alarms go off. But sometimes this works to my advantage. One day when the air raid alarms went off, the bomb shelter took a direct hit and all of the people in it were killed.

The other Jewish prisoners and I had to dig out the ruins and remove the bodies. It was horrible, and of course I didn't want the non-Jewish prisoners to be killed. But I must admit that I was thankful for not being allowed to take shelter with them. It is as if God took revenge on those Nazi dogs for not wanting us Jews to be safe.

I have already told you about one of the other harsh rules the Germans have: if a prisoner escapes, 10 other, totally innocent prisoners are executed. But I haven't told you that if a prisoner is missing right after the camp has been bombed, it is assumed that he was killed and is buried in the rubble. In this case, no other prisoners are killed.

This of course immediately sparked an idea in my pea brain. The next time the sirens go off, I told myself, I can escape with a clear conscience. And that's just what I did. When the alarm sirens went off, I took advantage of the confusion and made my way outside of the fence and was suddenly free. All I had to do was wait for the Allied planes to drop some bombs so that my conscience would be clear and no prisoners would be executed because of my escape. But as luck would have it, the planes flew over the camp without dropping any bombs.

Now I was faced with a dilemma. I was outside of the fence—free! But should I save *my* ass and allow 10 people to be executed, or should I return and wait for another opportunity? The answer of course was a no-brainer. I returned to my post at work without telling anyone what I almost did. And on our long march back to the barracks, I thought about the burden of the choices I had to make and the circumstances I was in. I was relieved that in the end I made the right choice.

It's a few nights later and I wake up and hear someone trying to steal our daily food ration from the cupboard by our bed. Immediately,

I start to yell at the culprit, who turns out to be a feeble old man. My outburst in turn wakes many of the prisoners, my father among them. But instead of yelling too, my father scolds me for being disrespectful and embarrassing the old man in public. He explains that the shame I brought on the old man far exceeded the value of one day's ration. He says I have tarnished the old man's reputation forever.

I challenge my father: "Are you telling me that it is okay for him to steal our rations but it is not okay for me to yell at him when I catch him in the act of stealing?"

"No, it is absolutely not okay for him to steal" my father says, "but this does not justify you embarrassing him in front of a room full of people. You need to think about the consequences before you act!"

I don't understand. Why does he think I shouldn't yell? Maybe it's just because my father is from another generation. But I do think he's right when he says, "You need to think about the consequences before you act!" If I had thought about the consequences the other day when I tried to escape during the air raid, I might never have tried at all. I realize that I am very lucky to have my father here because he gives me wisdom I otherwise would not have.

On the other hand, I must say that "thinking about consequences" can be dangerous, considering the conditions we live in. There are many times when spontaneous action would make the difference between life and death.

The Yom Kippur Hangings and Other Matters

How would you like to line up for hours, listening to a German prison official recite the "crimes" certain prisoners have committed? How would you like to be forced to watch the Germans hang these poor fellows by the neck. Because that's what we have to do, so the Germans can keep us in line and teach us how to obey the rules.

The worst of these public executions took place on September 1, 1944, the night of Yom Kippur (the Jewish Day of Atonement). They no doubt chose this day because it is our most sacred holiday, when all religious Jews fast to make amends for their sins. That day, the Nazis had the entire camp population line up for hours while they erected a gallows. This was the "stage" on which they would punish three prisoners who had tried to escape.

By the time all their preparations were completed, it was pitch dark outside. Even so, we could clearly see a thick rope with three nooses on it hanging from a hook. The entire stage was lighted by floodlights from the watch towers. As the executioners called out their numbers, the three prisoners were led onto the stage. Then, while they were being blindfolded, the camp commander read out the charges (attempted to escape) and the sentence (death by hanging). Afterwards, one prisoner was helped to climb on top of the bench and a noose was put around his neck. This process was repeated until all three men were standing on the bench silhouetted by spotlights. Then the camp commander addressed the 4,800 prisoners who had been standing for hours to witness this cruel spectacle: *"If any one of you attempts to escape,"* he said, *"you will end up on these gallows."* Immediately, the bench was pulled out from under the men's feet, leaving their bodies dangling and swinging from side to side, the two outside bodies slamming against the middle one.

Suddenly the rope broke loose and the victims fell onto the stage alive. A murmur of relief spread like lighting through the 4,800 prisoners who were forced to watch. I later heard that many hoped the Nazis would honor international law and grant the three prisoners a pardon. This law clearly states that you cannot execute a prisoner twice for the same crime. But the Nazis immediately proceeded to hang each prisoner again—this time one by one from the center hook.

That night we went back to our barracks wrapped in an eerie silence. This was supposed to be a time of great hope, a time when it looked like the Allies were winning and the Germans were being defeated. Yet here in the concentration camp, all of us were in great despair wondering if we would live long enough to see the end of the war.

The next morning, the wake-up call came as usual. It was as if the hangings had never happened. The prisoners were preoccupied with the daily routine of getting ready to report for the work lineup, being shackled and handcuffed and marching to the *Baustelle*. Only the orchestra took note of yesterday's events by playing sad Jewish and Gypsy tunes. That night when my father returned to the barrack after a hard day of work and fasting for Yom Kippur, I didn't say a word to him. I just wanted him to finally have something to eat. But I hadn't fasted because I thought, *Why should we punish our bodies even more than the Germans do? Fasting will only weaken us, and I felt no need to atone for sins I didn't commit.*

That evening I finally had a serious conversation with my father. This is how it went:

67

Me: I want to know how the hell 4,800 people can stand idly by when three of their fellow prisoners are being hanged. When the rope ripped off the hook and the prisoners had another chance to live, why did none of these 4,800 people come to their rescue? I would have expected to see a stampede of people running towards them in joy that their lives were saved. Yes, the Nazi guards in the watchtowers had their fingers on the triggers of their machine guns, but wouldn't it be worth a few dozen lives just to demonstrate to the Germans that we will not tolerate this kind of degradation? Let's face it, we are all starving to death anyway. We may just as well die as heroes the way those rebellious young men and women died in the Warsaw Ghetto.

Father: My dear son, we are powerless to accomplish anything much by sacrificing that many people, who may have a chance to survive the war. We cannot overpower the Nazis when they have so many weapons. The best we can do is have faith and pray to God that he will rescue us from this situation.

Me: But is it really necessary to be religious to be an optimist? Can't a person be an optimist without being religious?

Father: Let me tell you the story of two flies.

Me: *(Oh, boy, I've heard this one a hundred times before.)*

Father: Two flies fell into a big bowl of cream. One was an optimist and the other a pessimist. The pessimist lost all hope and had no faith in God or himself, so he just stopped flapping his wings and drowned in the cream. The optimist had a lot of faith in God and himself, so he kept flapping his wings until he made butter out of the cream and got out!"

I've heard this story so often I almost believe it—except for one thing. When you leave God out of the equation, optimism still works.

I share many of my experiences and thoughts with my father, but there are some I just can't talk about. (I'm sure you know what I mean.) Awhile after the Yom Kippur hangings, I had two experiences that made me realize I am no longer a child. One was pleasant, the other definitely not.

The *Baustelle,* with its thousands of foreign nationals, is a fascinating place that offers unexpected diversions. For several days I was working in a trench that was covered with wooden planks spaced an inch apart. The planks served as a bridge, and people were constantly walking back and forth over our heads. Usually I ignored them, but one day I saw a group of Italian girls start over. They were wearing skirts, and as they continued across the planks I got an unobstructed view of their bare legs. My reaction let me know in no uncertain terms that I was becoming a man. This was not a topic I discussed with my father, although I wish I could have because I needed to know what was happening to me.

Another incident was very troubling. One of the British prisoners of war was a man I had spoken to several times in German. One day he grabbed me by the arm and dragged me into a latrine, where he tried to rape me. It was a very awkward situation for me because I had developed a trusting relationship with him and now he was trying to rip off my pants.

At this point I didn't care if I got punished by the Nazis, I just started to scream and squirm until he finally let go of me. Afterwards, I was in total shock about the entire episode and at a loss to know what to do next.

For quite a while I didn't tell anyone, certainly not my father. I needed time to think about what happened and why. After several days I came to the conclusion that there is no point in judging the British prisoner of war harshly or being angry. I decided that he acted the way he did because of the desperate conditions we all find ourselves in. I just made sure to avoid him in the future.

During a Harsh Winter
a Miracle Happens

Now it is late autumn of 1943, and the days are getting shorter. The weather is cold, and we've even had a couple of snowstorms. Now our blue and white striped uniforms are too thin to protect us and as the snow accumulates on the ground it sticks to the wooden soles of our shoes and makes it hard to walk and maintain our balance. I can't see how we'll survive if we don't have warmer clothing and other shoes.

Luckily, through a mishmash of languages and a great many comical gestures, I manage to get some warm woolen sweaters through my contacts with the French prisoners of war. Of course, Father and I must be very careful to hide them. The punishment for wearing anything other than camp-issue clothing is 25 lashes on your bare bottom. Once before I had a sore rear end for days after receiving 25 lashes for smuggling in some bread, and I certainly don't want to go through that again! So we wear the sweaters under our uniforms and hope that the Germans don't discover them.

Our French contacts also found some leather shoes to replace our wooden ones. Let's just hope the Germans don't see them. Actually, I'm not too worried, because my pants are baggy enough to cover my feet, but I worry about my father.

Many other prisoners are not as lucky as we are. The lack of warm winter clothing brings on an outbreak of flu and pneumonia that spreads through the camp. Most prisoners are now so painfully thin they have no strength to fight it. They just go to the infirmary, where they are injected with cyanide poison and put out of their misery.

There are so many of them that the crematorium is now in operation around the clock and the sickening smoky smell of burning human flesh fills the air night and day. Because our barrack is right next to the crematorium, we cannot get away from it except when we are at work. The stench serves as a grim reminder of where we may all wind up.

The crematorium ovens at Blechhammer are in use night and day right next to our barrack, and the stench of burning flesh is always with us.

Despite all of this, there is a glimmer of hope for those of us who can survive until the end of the war. Lately I have given a great deal of thought to this and to the idea of escaping. But the more I think about it, the more I realize escape just wouldn't work. This is the case for a number of reasons. First, I don't have any civilian clothing, which I would need in order to disguise my identity on the outside. Second, I have nowhere to go where I would be hidden from the *Gestapo* (the German Secret Police). Third, it would put Father—and probably other prisoners—in danger. I guess I've learned well Father's lesson: *think before you act.*

At last I make up my mind. As long as my actions don't affect other people, I'm at liberty to exercise my judgment and do whatever I want. And then I think, *A normal 14-year-old would never have to face such a question, but these times are anything but normal.* And after that I think, *What if I had acted on the advice Uncle Moses gave me at the age of 9? What if I had left for Palestine at the age of 10? I probably would have been going to school and getting a normal education instead of rotting in a concentration camp with other European Jews. Would have, should have—I have to live in the present, take one day at a time and survive the war. Then I can make my way to the Promised Land.*

Being in the present is terrible, but it can also be boring as hell. The only thing that breaks the monotony is the frequent sound of air raid sirens, because it gives us hope that the Allies' planes will drop bombs on the camp.

Most of the time, they just fly over us without dropping any bombs, but the air raids also give us a break from work when we Jews can get together with the foreign prisoners of war and learn about the Allies' progress in fighting the Germans.

As I told you, my father keeps saying, "Have faith and hope." And I have sometimes told him, "Hope is the mother of fools," to which *he* replies, "Isn't it better to be a fool and survive than be a pessimist and die? You have to keep hoping for the best, and good things will happen to you." Well, something good just happened, and it makes me wonder if my father can see into the future.

Today is a frigid day in the new year, 1944, and the whole time I was working outdoors, I was completely miserable. But as we were walking, back from the *Baustelle* in shackles and handcuffs, I saw in the distance the outline of a woman who was walking on the side of the road in the same direction we were going. As we got closer to her, I thought *I recognize the coat she's wearing. It's just like the one my mother wore!* As we passed the woman, I had a chance to look at her face, and I was sure she was my mother. I poked the inmate to my right with my elbow and told him excitedly, "This woman is my mother!" He turned to me and hissed, "Keep it quiet. Otherwise, you may reveal her identity to the guards and put her in danger."

I did what he said, but my heart was pounding like a drum. I couldn't wait to get to the barrack and tell my father, but it turned out he was way ahead of me. He said that my mother had somehow been able to slip a note with her name and address on it to someone in his work group as they were walking by her.

This was a miracle! We just couldn't believe that she was able to do it without being noticed by the guards.

Well, it wasn't long before the entire camp was buzzing about this brave woman who was trying to make contact with her husband. But it also wasn't long before the *capos* got wind of it, and that worried us a lot. We were afraid that they would squeal to the Nazis, and then we would be in deep trouble.

Now the *capos* are aware of what my mother did, and they are concerned that my father may try to escape. They are not going to allow him to go to the *Baustelle* tomorrow morning. Instead he will do camp duty. And now other prisoners are worried that *they* will be punished if Father tries to escape. Of course, they don't know my father like I do. He would never jeopardize the lives of other people to save his own.

It's morning, and everyone has calmed down, but Father and I have unfinished business: we need to find a way to stay in contact with Mother without talking to her directly. We know that she is calling herself Barbara Zigmund, a typical German name that's not too different from her maiden name, Baila Siegman. We also know that she speaks German like a native. And we know that she works in a Catholic convent and passes herself off as an Aryan (non-Jewish) woman.

When Father is taken off camp duty and gets back to the *Baustelle,* he will talk to his civilian contacts and get some of his friends to talk to *their* contacts to see if he can find a reliable person who can stay in touch with Mother.

I will do the same, but it's complicated. We don't like to reveal her identity and whereabouts to total strangers, because we don't know if we can trust them.

Father's search for a trustworthy person to maintain contact between my mother and us has gone on for quite awhile without success. A few days ago, I finally asked him if it wouldn't be a good idea for me to ask my boss, Herr Frank, if he would be willing to do it for us. If he were, it would be the perfect solution to our problem. Father said he needed to give the idea some thought, but yesterday he agreed that it might work.

The question now is how do I approach Herr Frank? Father has given it some more thought and suggested that I talk to him about a hypothetical situation. I would say to him, "If I suddenly discovered that an aunt of mine is working on falsified Aryan identity papers in Gleiwitz, (a town in the vicinity of my mothers' location), would you be willing to contact her and tell her that we are alive?" It sounded like a great idea and certainly worth trying. Depending on his answer, we will decide how to handle the situation.

By now I feel very comfortable with Herr Frank, who often badmouths the Nazis and their war to me. Nevertheless, it will take a leap of faith to put my mother's welfare into someone else's hands. It will be one of the toughest tasks I've ever had to handle, and I want to make 100 percent sure that I'm doing it right.

Today's the day, and I'm so nervous. The hours drag on, but finally in the afternoon, while we're taking a break, I pose my question to my boss very innocently.

"Herr Frank, if I suddenly found out that an aunt of mine is working for a German farmer near Gleiwitz, would you help me keep in contact with her?"

"Sure" he answers. I would be delighted to do that for you!"

I thank him for being so kind and generous, and when I get back to camp I tell my father, word for word, what happened. I say I believed what Herr Frank said, and Father agrees that we must trust him. We are fully aware that being able to stay in contact with Mother will greatly improve our chances of staying alive until this terrible war is over.

Just before we line up for our bowls of soup, Father–being in some ways a typical father–points out the obvious to me: "Let this be a lesson to you. Never lose hope."

Now, of course, it's up to me to decide when and how to tell Herr Frank the *real* story.

The following week I get up the courage to raise the subject with Herr Frank again. This time I tell him the entire story–how Mother trudged through the snow alongside Father's work group and slipped her address to someone. When I finish, his face lights up and he pulls me over to him, hugs me and says, "This *real story* of yours doesn't change my mind a bit. I will be happy to do it for you."

I laugh as I give him her name and address and watch his face to see his reaction. You see, Mother doesn't really live in Gleiwitz but in Neisse-Neustadt, which is about 30 kilometers (18½ miles) east of there. But Herr Frank doesn't care. He says that unless the weather is too bad, he will ride there on his motorcycle on Sunday.

This whole weekend, Father and I have been on pins and needles, anxiously looking forward to Monday, when we will go to work at the *Baustelle*. I have been amazed at how my outlook on life has changed. Before, I was filled with despair, but now I am a convert to *hope*. Skirmishes in the soup line don't bother me; I am even able to shrug off harassment by the *capos*. It feels as if I have been injected with a new spirit of anticipation for the day when this war will finally end.

At the same time, my own good fortune makes me much more aware of the plight of the other inmates, who have lost all hope and all reasons for living. Once an inmate has nothing to live for, everything in him and around him leads to the path of self-destruction and death. I feel terrible for the other prisoners, but I am thankful to have learned some important lessons from my experiences. Living in hell every day makes it hard to stand back and look at things objectively. In my case, it took an extraordinary event to get me to a point where I could *be* objective, and I am so thankful to have had that opportunity.

It's Monday morning, and Father and I can hardly wait to line up and go to the *Baustelle*. All I can think of is seeing Herr Frank and finding out about his meeting with my mother. Every minute of the march seems like an hour, but at last I arrive at my workstation.

But where is Herr Frank? I climb up the steel girders with the speed of a monkey to see if I can catch a glimpse of him. At last, there he is in the distance. At first he doesn't see me, but then he does and he has this smirk on his face that says, as clearly as any words could, *mission accomplished!*

As soon as he reaches our workstation, he takes me aside behind the welding machine so that no one can see us. Then he gives me a letter that my mother wrote to my father—and some food. I don't quite know how to thank him for his good deed, but I blurt out a few words.

"Oh, no," he says, "the pleasure was all mine. I was just glad I could help."

But I know that it was an *enormous* favor he did for us and I will always be grateful to him for doing it. More than that, the fact that he took such a huge a risk to help us out gives me food for thought. Now I realize that it is unfair to condemn a whole group of people for the wrongful acts of some. I used to generalize that all Germans are bad. Now I will have to bite my tongue.

I have had to hide the food that Mother sent us under my striped uniform so no one can see it. It made me nervous all day, so as we passed the entrance gate back at camp I was filled with relief and rushed to the barrack where my father was waiting anxiously for me. The barrack was full of men, but I managed to slip the letter to him and quickly place the food under my mattress when nobody was looking. Then we went outside, where Father could read the letter in private.

The letter gave us a detailed description of what happened in Shrodula after we were separated from Mother. She described in detail the horrors that she witnessed while waiting in the selection line. She also told us that my brother Benek was torn away from her by the

Nazis and sent to the gas chambers in Auschwitz-Birkenau. Then she explained how she escaped. It seems that Mother was selected by the Nazis to help gather all the clothing and valuables left behind by the residents of the ghetto where we lived. While doing that job, she went to the hospital to see if there was anything she could do for our sister Rachel. But when she got there, she learned that Rachel had been sent to Auschwitz the day before. Mother said that she herself escaped because her job gave her a chance to get papers that identified her as an Aryan.

In closing, she said she prayed that someday we could be reunited and rebuild our family.

As my father was reading the letter, scenes from our lives were racing through my mind: the family meeting at which we all promised to take care of our sister when her leg was amputated, my mother's anguished face when my brother Benek was ripped from her arms and sent to Auschwitz-Birkenau, her screams when she found out that Rachel had been taken to Auschwitz.

Yet with all this pain and suffering, she was able to gather the courage and strength to deliver a note containing her address to a marching column of concentration camp inmates. She had the audacity to express her longing to meet with my father and rebuild our family. I will always see her walking in the deep snow with determination and purpose. I will always see her as a devoted wife and mother and a valiant woman. These are the bittersweet aspects of life that make it worth living.

I'm on an
Emotional Roller Coaster

Weeks have passed and nothing in our immediate environment has changed. The same old boring routine repeats itself every day: the lineups, the shoving and pushing, the harassment of prisoners by *capos*, the orchestra. The only thing that is different is me. I believe my new attitude is enough to pull me through any rough spots I may encounter, and I must tell you the rough spots keep getting rougher.

Conditions in camp are getting worse at an alarming pace. Sickness, malnutrition, frostbite, pneumonia and diarrhea have reached epidemic proportions. There is no more room in the infirmary, so the sick are taken straight from the barracks to the crematorium.

These days the stench of burning flesh is everywhere–there's no getting away from it. In these conditions it is very hard not to be deeply affected by the plight of my fellow prisoners.

Despite the sickness and death of so many people in camp, the production quotas the German authorities set up for us at the *Baustelle* don't change. They stand over those of us who are left and watch our every step. They threaten us with swift punishment if we don't meet their quotas.

Now the air raid sirens sound all day long, and bombing is much more frequent. It tells us that the Allied air forces rule the skies.

Meanwhile, the German anti-aircraft batteries are a joke. They frequently go off long *after* the Allied planes are gone, and it's obvious that the German radar system isn't working.

More than that, we can really see that there is a crack in the Germans' accuracy and discipline. They have begun to lose their feelings of superiority and sometimes have actual conversations with the foreign workers. Loyalty to the great Herr Hitler has started to fall apart at the seams.

As time goes on, I am on more and more of an emotional roller coaster, with the peaks and valleys coming in shorter and shorter intervals. I cannot seem to find a middle ground no matter how hard I try, and at times I even think about suicide. After all, what's the point of living like this? Again, I turn to my father for advice, and again he tells me, "There is absolutely nothing you can do to change the situation you are in. You must learn to accept it and cope with it the best you can."

Then he points out, "You must be aware that we are far better off than the rest of the prisoners in this camp. We discovered that your mother is alive, and we are staying in contact with her. We are getting food packages that none of the other prisoners have. We are receiving letters of encouragement and love. You have all the reason in the world to have faith and hope that you will live to see the end of the war soon. All you need is patience."

"How can you be patient when hundreds of people are having their intestines attacked by dysentery, when this horrible disease is killing hundreds of people all around you? People are dying like flies and there is no help in sight. How can *I* be patient when I'm constantly staring death in the face—when I never know if it will be my turn next?"

But no matter how much I rage, my father never lets up or gives up on me. He just keeps saying that I need to be thankful and count my blessings and concentrate on seeing the light at the end of the tunnel. Concentrate on how I can survive and live to see the end of the war.

Think of the day when we will be liberated and join Mother to build a new life.

"Maybe your older brother Moses David will survive the war and join us," he says. "Maybe you will be able to fulfill your dream and join the Zionist pioneers in the *Promised Land*. Wouldn't that be something to look forward to?"

Now months have passed. It is November of 1944, and I am beginning to feel uncomfortable asking Herr Frank to go to my mother so often. I discussed this problem with my father and we decided that he would try to get some contacts through people he knows in his work group.

There are a number of drawbacks to getting people from the concentration camp involved. For one thing, the more who are involved, the greater the risk of exposure. Also, we would have to share all of Mother's food packages with the prisoners who help us. After considering all the facts, we have decided to stick with the arrangement we already have. After all, it seems to be working quite well.

This—and the hope that the war will end soon—has put me in a much better mood. For one thing, we have heard that the Allied forces are actually fighting on German soil. The Russian army is at the gates of Breslau, and General Dwight Eisenhower from the United States and General Montgomery of Britain are advancing on two fronts from the West. This has filled the prisoners of war at the *Baustelle* with joy. Every day they give us updates about the amazing advances being made against the Germans. They even say that this will be their last Christmas and New Year in captivity.

At the industrial complex the air raid sirens are constantly blaring, but we no longer see Americans dropping the bombs; now it is Russian bombers escorted by Russian fighter planes. While the bombers drop their bombs, the fighter planes dive to attack the Germans' anti-aircraft batteries. And now there isn't a single German plane in the air. It appears to us that the German Air Force has been totally destroyed.

Some time has elapsed, but so far we've only seen a few snowflakes, and they have not been sticking to the ground. Even so, it has gotten cold enough for even more people, in their weakened condition, to catch colds and get pneumonia. Already, many have died. Yet even sickness and death have not reduced the overall air of optimism in the *Baustelle.*

However, the mood of the concentration camp prisoners is much more subdued than it was a short time ago. While we look forward to the war ending, we don't know what to expect once we get liberated. We know of the inhuman things the Nazis have done in the occupied countries of Europe. We know that they have tried to exterminate all the Jews in Europe. But we don't know what they have achieved. We don't know what to expect once we get "home" or even if we will have homes to go to. This weighs heavily on everyone's heart.

It's past the middle of January 1945, and our fear of the unknown has increased. Each day, we leave the barbed-wire gates of our camp and march to the music of the orchestra, just as we always have. But the rest of the way to the *Baustelle*, we are accompanied by the sound of distant artillery fire. It has been going on like this for several weeks, and it makes us wonder, *Why are the Russians not coming to liberate us?* We know that Blechhammer is close to the Oder River, where the Germans will most likely set up a line of defense to stop the Russian troops. But where *are* those troops?

The Death March

The Nazi regime of the Third Reich is on the threshold of total collapse, and the Nazi leadership has decided to empty all the concentration camps that are in the path of the advancing Russian army. They want to erase any traces of the terrible things that they have done, but they also want to take us prisoners deeper into Germany, where they will use us to build defensive fortifications for the retreating German army. For many of the prisoners, it will be their death march.

Today, January 21, 1945, started out like any other Sunday. We prisoners were busy with our cleaning chores, busy getting ready for another work week. The sounds of artillery fire and explosions were loud and clear. The stench of burning human flesh filled the air, especially in our barrack, #15, which is next to a wall of the crematorium.

At 10:30 a.m. a rumor started spreading all over camp that we were going to be forced to evacuate, but no one knew when it would happen or where we would be taken. At about 11:00 a.m. the *capos* were running around with their bullhorns, ordering all prisoners to report at the *Appellplatz* with all of our belongings by 12:00 noon.

Normally an announcement like this would come over the loudspeaker system, and immediately afterwards Nazi guards and *capos* would force us into action. This time there wasn't a Nazi guard in sight.

Now, another rumor began to spread: the Nazis had left the food storage facilities unguarded. As soon as I got word of this, I joined the crowd and got away with a carton full of food–mostly bread and margarine–and brought it to my father in the barrack.

Father and I knew that joining the evacuation would only prolong our suffering, so at first we considered hiding in the attic of the barrack with the provisions I had stolen and waiting for the war to end. I was in favor of this idea, but Father argued against it, saying that the Germans would most likely dynamite the crematorium next to our barrack. When that happened, we would be discovered and shot. His argument made sense.

Meanwhile, the Nazis had the *capos* issue warnings on their bullhorns: *Any prisoner found hiding or not reporting for the evacuation will be shot on the spot.*

Then Father and I thought, *Could the two of us escape during the evacuation and join my mother at the Catholic convent where she works?* We had definite advantages over the other prisoners. We had leather shoes, woolen sweaters and woolen hats with earmuffs. We had the bread and margarine that I had managed to steal. All we had to do was hide it well enough that the Germans and our fellow prisoners didn't notice it. We decided to do this, and concealed everything as best we could.

At about 11:45 a column of heavily armed SS vehicles loaded with officers and guards entered the camp and drove straight to the *Appellplatz*. The loudspeakers began blaring orders for all of us to assemble and warning, *Anyone hiding or failing to report for the evacuation will be shot on the spot.* By this time, Father and I had all our food hidden under our clothing and tied down with strings so that it would not be noticed. The only things that could be seen were the canisters and blankets we had been ordered to carry.

As soon as we were ready, we walked over to the assembly place, where the prisoners were lined up in rows five deep. This time we weren't shackled or handcuffed.

After the *capos* took roll call, the SS camp commander addressed us on the loud speaker: *This evacuation has been ordered to ensure your safety. You are going to a more secure place with better conditions.* That certainly sounded like the line they used on women and children before sending them to their deaths in the showers at Birkenau.

Now we are ready to march. Rows of SS guards with horse-drawn sleds and dogs at their sides are waiting to take up their positions. This is another instance when the fate of over 4,000 people rests in the hands of these evil Nazis.

"MARCH!" bellows the SS commander, and a vast column of people in rows of five across begins to move. In the lead is an SS guard on a sled, and alongside of us are the other SS guards.

As the column moves towards the camp gates, I notice the members of the orchestra have blankets over their shoulders and tin canisters hanging at their waists. The music they play is sad, reflecting the mood of the prisoners. Suddenly, the silence of the marchers is broken by the camp commander as he shouts an order.

As we walk out onto the road, Father and I see that the snow is building up on the wooden soles of the other prisoners' shoes. When we walked to the *Baustelle,* we were shackled and cuffed to each other. This kept the inmates with wooden-soled shoes from wobbling and falling. Now, without the help of shackles and cuffs, prisoners are wobbling, and this slows everybody down. As soon as the SS guards see this, they order their dogs to attack. I guess they think this will help!

The Nazis, in their great wisdom, have not provided us with Port-a-Potties. If we have to go, they allow us to relieve ourselves on the side of the road, but we have to return to our places in line *running* if we don't want to be mauled by their dogs. These SS guards like nothing better than seeing their dogs attack a prisoner. You must have to be a psychopath to qualify for their job!

The longer we march, the more people we lose. One minute they're walking with us, and the next they're falling by the side of the road. Once they lag behind us, we have no way of knowing what has happened to them.

The road we're marching on is the main highway, which is crowded with military convoys going in both directions. Going east towards the front lines are trucks loaded with ammunition and supplies, dragging artillery pieces behind them. Going west are many empty trucks and military ambulances. Also, there are German civilians heading west to escape the Russians. They have abandoned their villages and towns in fear of the Russians and travel on foot, in cars or on horse-drawn sleds, heading towards the territory the Americans now occupy.

As the sky gets darker, we begin to wonder if they plan to have us march all night. We don't have to wonder for long, though, because now we're veering off the main highway onto a side road that leads to a village. As we enter it, we see that the place is totally deserted.

Suddenly we are being pushed from behind by other prisoners, but we don't know why. Almost immediately the pushing and shoving turns into a stampede headed towards a set of open barn doors. Now, people are falling and being trampled because the SS are whipping everyone into a frenzy, trying to shove as many people as they can into the barn.

The sad result of our stampede is that many people are horribly injured and some are stomped to death before the barn doors are closed and locked for the night. All around us we can hear the moans of people who were run over by their fellow prisoners, but these moans gradually stop as the injured die or pass out from exhaustion.

My father and I are fortunate to have found a spot on a haystack where we can sit—fortunate because we are packed into the barn like sardines in a can.

As we marched today, we hoped that the Germans would give us some food and water to drink, but we should have known better. Instead, they locked us in for the night and forgot all about us.

As it becomes quiet, Father and I share some of the food I was able to steal from the warehouse. We have to do it very quietly in order not to attract the attention of the other prisoners who are still awake, but it's not easy when you are packed so close together.

Outside, the wind is howling through the cracks in the barn, but luckily we have blankets to cover our bodies and conceal our food. The only advantage of being squeezed in so tightly is that the warmth generated by our bodies keeps us from freezing.

By now, most everyone has fallen into a deep sleep, but my mind is racing. I want to try to escape, but I need to talk to Father about it. It's impossible here in this barn, but I will try to broach the idea to him tomorrow while we are walking.

At the first light of dawn, the sirens start blasting from the German trucks, ordering us to line up for the day's march. As we get near the barn doors, we notice that the corpses of people who were trampled the night before are strewn around outside. Yet the prisoners are too miserable to look at them; they just follow the orders to line up.

Outside, it is so cold we nearly freeze while we wait for all the prisoners to assemble. We keep hoping that the Germans will give us some hot tea or soup, but there is nothing—no food, no water, nothing.

While we are waiting, Father and I decide to pack our tin canisters with snow so that we can melt it to water on our bodies. Otherwise we will die of dehydration.

Now the SS guards are taking up their positions on both sides of us, and the orders to march are shouted out. As the column winds through the village to the main highway, we see that it is still packed with German civilians trying to flee from the Russians.

Millions of Russians died during the German occupation of their territories, and the Germans know it's payback time. That's why they are fleeing for their lives. Today, though, they are barely able to move. The civilian traffic and the military convoys on the highway have slowed the pace of the march.

This is our second day without food or water. The prisoners who were suffering from starvation and malnutrition *before* the march began, are having trouble holding on to life. The eyes of some prisoners bulge and they begin to babble. Others are stricken by dysentery and diarrhea. Often they go to the side of the road, pull their pants down in a desperate attempt to relieve themselves and die on top of their own filth. Others lie down on the side of the road and freeze to death with their blankets on their shoulders and their tin canisters by their sides.

While we are dragging ourselves along, I finally have a chance to talk with my father. First, I take a piece of bread and margarine out of the stash I have stored in my pants and share it with him. I've gotten quite warm during the march, so I tell him that my blanket is getting in my way—I will get rid of it and pick up another from one of the dead bodies in the late afternoon. I tell him that unless we take a chance and hide ourselves in the hay in the next few days, we will wind up like these people, as corpses on the side of the road. I tell him that I think we should try to escape. I look in his eyes for a minute, but he does not respond, which I interpret to mean D*o what you have to do, but don't look for my approval.*

As we trudge on, I toss my blanket onto the side of the road and find that it really makes walking a lot easier. Then I look at my father and point to the people strewn on the side of the road.

"If I ever survive this war," I tell him, "I have an obligation to these martyrs and to Uncle Moses. I have to make my way to the Promised Land and help end, once and for all, the persecution of the Jews." He looks at me with tears in his eyes and says, "From your mouth to God's ears."

We hug and my own eyes fill with tears. I know that my father's love, wisdom and understanding during our last fight for survival are priceless. They have given me the will to live, something I will cherish for the rest of my life. My father is my pillar of strength and I love him deeply.

We keep on walking until the skies get dark, and once again it becomes clear that we will soon veer off the main highway to another abandoned village. When the guards aren't looking, I step to the side of the column and pull a blanket off one of the dead prisoners who lies beside the road. I feel awful, but right now my own survival must be my main concern.

This time the push to the barn is much stronger as the Nazis whip the prisoners to create a stampede. The first men who are shoved into the barn fall and are trampled to death by the wave of people behind them. The rest of us just collapse on the hay in total exhaustion.

This morning the sirens wake us up before the crack of dawn. Father and I don't have a chance to hide in the hay. As if that isn't enough, when I start to get up I realize that our stash of food has been stolen.

Frantically, I turn to my father and ask him, "What do we do now?" His answer is, "We are in God's hands."

Now the guards are rushing us and there is no time to talk, so like obedient cows we join the rest of the herd to line up. Luckily the snow in our canisters has melted and we are able to have a drink of water.

I also realize that I have a few slices of bread with margarine in my back pants pocket. When no one is looking, I divide it into several portions to keep us going as long as possible. It certainly isn't enough to live on but enough to keep us from dying. That is more than anyone else has.

Now the order to march is given. But when we reach the main highway today, we see a sight that amazes us. Russian planes are attacking the German military columns on the highway, and German civilians are running for cover into the snowy fields. Until the planes fly away, there is total chaos.

As things get back to normal, we begin our march again. Although it was nice for a change to see Germans running for their lives, it has not altered our situation in any way. The Nazi guards are just getting nastier.

Not that it does them any good. Today, more people are stumbling to the side of the road and dying. The rest of us are now forced to move to the side of the road and stop marching more and more often.

When we stop walking, we are able to see that the German military trucks going by are loaded with teenage soldiers. The "masters of the world" are now sending the Hitler *Yugend* (Youth) to the front lines to make a last stand.

While we wait for the convoys to pass, we finish drinking the water in our canisters and repack them with fresh snow from the side of the road. A fully packed canister of snow barely yields a quarter canister of water, so we have to repeat this process quite often in order to keep ourselves alive.

We have started our march again, and to us it seems endless. "How can the Germans possibly want to use us to dig trenches and make fortifications for them when they are starving us to death?" I ask my father. His answer is, "Do you really expect logic and reasonable thinking from beasts like the Nazis? Don't expect anything from them and you won't be disappointed!"

While we are talking, I ask him again about hiding in the hay tonight. He says that first we must get an idea of where we are in relation to the village where my mother is located. Otherwise, we will be wandering around in a strange place and be handed over to the Nazis, who will execute us on the spot. Nevertheless, I feel that at some point we have to take a chance and escape. Otherwise we will die of starvation or dysentery.

Night is approaching, and it's time for me to grab a blanket from a dead prisoner before we leave the highway to find an abandoned village. As we turn off the main highway, a pair of Russian planes starts shelling the German convoys. Now people are running in all directions, and smoke and flames are billowing up from the convoys. But the Nazis keep us marching towards the village and whip anyone who turns around to see the slaughter.

By now, Father and I are familiar with the routine of the stampede and brace ourselves for it. Others apparently have the same idea, and tonight not as many people are trampled. As soon as we literally "hit the hay," we fall into a deep sleep. We don't even dare to take our treasured leather shoes off for fear that someone will steal them while we're asleep.

At the crack of dawn, the sirens go off and an SS guard stands at the barn door, rushing us to line up for the march. This is the fourth day and there is no end in sight.

Today it takes longer for all of the prisoners to assemble. Even the heartless SS guards seem to realize that by now these prisoners are a bunch of skeletons in their final stages of life.

At last, we get under way and plod to the main highway, but the column of prisoners is much shorter.

Before we enter the main highway, we must halt to allow several military convoys to pass. This gives us a chance to refill our canisters with snow. Now, it is getting more difficult to walk. I move along in a daze, as my mind wanders off somewhere and suddenly comes back to face reality. Now the hunger pangs gnaw at my stomach–I can think of nothing else–and I realize that I am starving. I also know that I'm coming down with something. I have a horrible pain in my gut and I feel like I'm going to throw up. I don't want to tell my father about it and get him worried, so I try hard to act as normal as possible.

What seems like hours later, we are walking by a German farm and suddenly I see the farmer toss at us a bucketful of small potatoes he has cooked for his hogs. The prisoners fall on the potatoes like a bunch of vultures.

I manage to catch a small one, which is still warm. To my shame, I hesitate before sharing it with my father. Immediately, I feel guilty for hesitating, but I feel proud that I am able to overcome my selfish instincts and share with my father. Starvation can make us humans act like animals.

The march begins again, and we pass a village. At the next intersection is a road sign with an arrow pointing in the same direction we are going. It says *Neisse-Neustadt 36 km*. Suddenly, I realize where we are: we're only 36 kilometers (22½ miles) away from where Mother is.

Now I tell my father, "This is our chance. We must *act*!"

"Thirty-six kilometers is a long way," he says. "We could be caught and executed many times over if we are not careful. And remember, we must make sure not jeopardize your mother's safety. We must be cautious and plan our escape very carefully."

This is enough to dampen my excitement for a while, but I'm certainly not ready to take no for an answer.

The daylight is dimming, and it's time to find another blanket before we turn off the highway. In the distance I see lights that must be the village we are going to.

As we turn off, all I can think of is trying to find a way to convince my father to escape, and I forget to check the sign at the crossroads that points to Neisse. My mind is racing, racing.

Now Father and I lock arms to brace ourselves against the stampede of prisoners from the rear of the column. But the shoving tonight is much weaker; people simply don't have the strength to push.

Inside, we flop down on the hay. While Father and I try to catch our breaths, I again make my case for escaping.

"Father," I begin, "at some point we *must* take a chance. Nobody is going to do it for us and time is running out. Our strength is gone. We have to do it *now*. We need to bury ourselves in the hay before the SS guards come around with their dogs and sirens."

But Father is still cautious. "Look," he says, "we are getting closer to Neisse all the time. Why don't we wait one more day and then see where we are?"

This is not what I want to hear. I say, "Okay, Father, we'll wait one more day, but then we must go for it! Putting it off gets us nowhere."

He doesn't reply, and I fall into a deep, peaceful sleep, hoping that we have finally made a decision to take action.

It's Now or Never

Today is Thursday, January 25, 1945. It is a day I will never forget. Before dawn, the sirens shriek. By the open doors of the barn, an SS guard with a dog at his side is holding a whip and yelling, *"Mach schnell, mach schnell* (hurry up, hurry up)."

There is a bone-chilling wind that makes everyone stamp their feet to keep from freezing. Today I will be glad to have a blanket to wrap around me. Once again, we pack our canisters with snow before the column begins to move.

This time, as we come to the main highway, I am unable to see the words on the road sign because the wind had covered it with snow. Father says he thinks we are walking in the direction of Neisse, but he can't be one 100 percent sure.

Even in this freezing weather the road is filled with German women and children running away from the Russians. There are few men–probably because they are serving in the German army. Overhead, Russian planes are flying low and attacking the military convoys, but they don't come close to us. I guess they must have recognized our concentration camp uniforms.

This is our fifth day marching nonstop without food or water, and the death rate has now reached into the hundreds. It is nearly impossible for us to keep up with the pace of the march. Most prisoners were walking skeletons to start with, and we have reached the limit of what the human body can endure. For all of us, the end of the war is so near and yet so far.

It has been terrifying for me to witness human suffering on such a massive scale, and now I too have started to have diarrhea. This scares the hell out of me, because I *know* that this is usually a death sentence. Just when I was looking for a miracle to happen, I find myself in a hopeless situation. Yet I don't want to tell my father and have him go through the pain of seeing me collapse in front of his eyes.

We've been marching for hours, and suddenly I see a road sign clearly marked *Neisse 24 km* (15 miles). With the little strength I have left, I turn to my father and say, "This is it. We must hide in the hay tonight. We cannot wait any longer."

When we are bedded down for the night, Father agrees to hide in the hay at the crack of dawn.

It is 5:00 a.m. on Friday, January 26, 1945. Outside, it is pitch black. The sirens pierce the air and two Nazi guards and a *capo* fling the barn gates wide open and begin rushing the prisoners to the lineup. Their flashlights are blinding; there's no way we can hide in the hay now. We must leave the barn with the rest of the prisoners and get in line.

Most of the prisoners are so weak they can barely move, but the Nazi guards beat them and their dogs attack them to speed things up. Meanwhile, Father and I wait in the bitter cold. On the horizon, the dawn is breaking and we are able to see which direction we will be going.

As the column starts to march towards the main highway, a squadron of Russian planes appears, silhouetted against the bright eastern sky. Soon afterward, we can feel the ground shaking and hear loud explosions in the distance.

At the main highway we are suddenly stopped, and again I can clearly see the road sign. It points to *Neisse—24 km* (15 miles) to our left. While we are waiting at the junction, Father asks 10 men to stay together so that he can conduct the *Shachris* (morning prayers) and say the *Kaddish* (the prayer said on the anniversary of a death). Father is doing this because today is the anniversary of my grandfather's death.

While my father is getting the men together and praying, I find out why the Nazis have stopped us here. German soldiers are leading a long column of French prisoners of war on the main highway in the direction of Neisse. And then *we* begin to move—but in the opposite direction!

On the side of the road to our left is a group of 11- to 13-year-old Hitler *Yugend* boys watching the spectacle of skeletons marching in blue and white striped uniforms. On the main road is the column of French prisoners of war. Suddenly, the SS man who is guarding us turns around with his back to us to search for something in his horse-drawn sled.

Now I can see the end of the column of French prisoners of war down the highway to my right. It's now or never! I quickly tear off my striped uniform and drop it on the ground. Now I'm dressed in my French woolen sweater and cap. I hurriedly poke my father's elbow while he is reciting the *Kaddish* and tell him in Yiddish *Tate, ich gei* (Dad, I'm going).

I walk right past the Hitler *Yugend* and straight towards the column of the French POWs. With my French sweater and cap, I can easily pass for one of them and get to Neisse to join my mother. There's only one problem: I am too *young* to be a French prisoner of war.

Suddenly I have these terrible cramps in my belly, and I know that I'm getting an attack of diarrhea. Luckily I'm able to run behind a snow bank on the side of the highway and get my pants down. And then my guts literally *gush* out of me.

I must have passed out. I don't know how long I've been lying in the snow or what made me wake up. Perhaps it was my grandfather's spirit working on my behalf. Who knows? I don't usually have thoughts like this, but right now I'm in a daze and feel like I have just been brought back from the dead.

From behind my snow bank I have a good view of the road, but no one can see me. All I can see is heavy civilian traffic and military convoys, but there is no sign of the French prisoners or the death march. Then I notice two Ukrainian soldiers and decide to approach them.

"Please," I beg, "please give me a piece of bread." Without a word, they pull some bread from their backpacks and hand it to me.

I thank them for the bread, but when I try to eat it, I realize that it is frozen. I am simply not strong enough to bite into it.

Now I am faced with a situation my father and I discussed frequently in the camp. *Careful planning is an essential part of a successful escape.* It's not only the escape itself; it's the aftermath that must be thought out in detail. As I am thinking this, I say to myself, *Bullshit – I would never have escaped if I had taken time out to think about it. There are situations in life when you have to act instinctively and go by your gut feelings or else you die.*

But now I have a more important thing to think about: how will I manage to get to my mother? The first thing I decide to do is to try and get lost in the crowd and keep on walking in the direction of Neisse.

There are thousands of people on the road, traveling by car, riding on horse-drawn sleds and walking. There should be no problem fitting into this crowd as long as no one talks to me. But there are also military convoys, and I'm worried that somebody might discover who I am.

Frequently, Russian planes dive down over the German convoys and shoot at the soldiers in them. Then the civilians run into the fields on the side of the road until the raid is over, and I run with them. Now that I no longer have my tin canister, I just eat snow to quench my thirst while we are there.

As we begin to move again, I realize how hungry I am. Before long, I smell the aroma of food being cooked. It is getting stronger and stronger. And then I turn around and notice a military field kitchen on a horse-drawn sled. In front is a bench where a German guard and a French prisoner are sitting. In the rear is a large kettle with burning coal underneath it and a stoop behind that.

I quickly step out of line and climb onto the rear stoop. Reaching over the kettle, I tap the cook on the shoulder and tell him in my broken French, "I'm a Jew. I just escaped from the march. Could you please give me a piece of bread?" The cook gives me a large bowl of hot soup and a large slice of bread with lots of melted cheese on top. I thank him several times and go to the side of the road to feast on this bounty.

I am at a total loss to describe the gratitude and satisfaction I feel while I am eating. The fact that my stomach is blowing up like a balloon because it is my first hot food in six days doesn't matter at all. What matters is having a heavenly experience with food. I only wish I could share my meal with my father.

Another Miracle

I can't tell you how much this meal has changed my mood and energy. As a horse-drawn sled with German peasants in it glides by, I grab hold and hang on for a few miles before they pull off the main road. As Russian planes continue to dive bomb the German convoys, I run back and forth into the fields for cover, along with the other civilians.

After one raid, a German woman starts talking to me. "The Jews are responsible for the war! They are financing all the armament industries of Russia and America," she says. On and on she goes, repeating the Nazi propaganda line word for word. I, of course, can't say a thing. I speak German with an obvious accent and don't want to raise any suspicions, so I just listen and keep walking along until another air raid forces us off the road and I lose sight of her.

When I return to the road, another woman starts a similar conversation with me. I listen politely, but when she tells me that her family has lived in this area for many generations, I ask her for directions to Neisse.

She tells me that Neisse is the name of a river that divides the town and says that nearby the German army is building fortifications to stop the Russian advance. She also gives me precise directions to Neisse-Neustadt. I thank her, and as soon as I get a chance I grab hold of the back of the next horse-drawn sled that is going in the right direction. On the outskirts of town, the sled veers onto a side road, so I hop off and walk into the town.

Neisse-Neustadt is almost deserted. The woman who gave me directions said I must cross the bridge in order to get to my mother's address, but I quickly see that there is a problem: this is where the German military is building fortifications around the river and a sentry is stationed on both sides of the river. I also see that I have no choice: I *have* to go across the bridge and face the sentry.

Now my mind begins to race, as I think of all the questions the sentry may ask me. When I get nearer the bridge, I also watch carefully to see how the guards are checking other people and vehicles. I have to give the impression that I belong in this area.

I get my courage up and head straight for the sentry booth. The guard stops me and asks, *"Ausweiss bitte* (Identification please). I tell him in German with a heavy French accent, "I am working for a German farmer on the outskirts of Gleiwitz (a town about 30 kilometers east of here). We were on a horse-drawn sled escaping the war zone, and during a Russian air raid we ran into the fields for cover. In the confusion, my boss and I became separated. Now I cannot find him, and *he* has all my papers. I'm looking for work now, so could you please direct me to an employment office in Neisse where they can assign me to a local farmer?"

It's a good story, if I do say so myself, but the guard just keeps repeating, "You must have your ID card with you." I act innocent and make believe that I have trouble understanding him. "All I want is to go to the employment office and get assigned to a job with a local farmer," I say.

We keep going at it back and forth, until he gets tired of me and motions with his arm across the bridge. "Get the hell lost," are the last words I hear as I quickstep across the bridge.

Wow! What a relief that was. I don't know how I got the nerve to carry on like that with the guard, except I *did* know that—unlike the SS—regular army guys like him are fairly easygoing and green. This is just another instance when I couldn't plan in advance – I just had to roll with the punches.

Now that I'm actually in the town where my mother is, I have to find #12 Cloister Strasse and the convent where my mother is working as an Aryan woman. Being born to an orthodox Jewish family, I have never been to a convent before. I don't know what one looks like and I have no idea what to expect once I get there.

In deciding whom to ask for directions, I want to make sure not to raise any suspicions that might pose a threat to my mother. I think a young teenager might be best. He might not be as suspicious as an adult. As soon as the thought crosses my mind, a young boy comes out into the street, so I go over to him and ask where Cloister Strasse 12 is. He points to the church and says that as soon as I pass it, I should turn right and I'll be there.

Sure enough, as I pass the church I see the sign *Cloister Strasse*, and as I turn right onto it I see an ornate wrought-iron fence with a decorative gate and the number 12.

Now my heart starts beating like a drum. I go through the gate and up to the building's carved main door. As I walk up the two granite steps leading to the door, I wonder if I should ring the bell or just knock on the door. But I decide instead to open the door quietly and take a peek to see what is going on inside.

By this time, my heart is beating double time. I grab the door handle and open the door just enough to see what is inside. What I see is a very large entry hall with wide floorboards of highly polished wood and a stairway with a beautiful wide wooden banister. On the left side of the door is a huge sculpture of Christ on the cross. There is such an eerie stillness in the place; I don't know quite what to make of it.

Before I step into the entry hall, I make sure that my shoes are clean and dry. Then I walk in and stand on the left side of the door, right under the cross, and wait for someone to come. While I wait, I think how ironic my situation is. Here I am, a persecuted Jew, seeking shelter under the very symbol that is responsible for many centuries of my people's persecution.

At last I see a lady dressed in a white uniform walk down the stairs and into another room. I don't know if she even saw me standing here.

So I wait in the eerie stillness a while longer until the same lady comes out of the room with a teakettle and a tray with cookies in her hands.

Before she starts back up the stairs, I call out to her in German, "Excuse me please!" As I say this, she turns around and comes towards me.

Now I ask her in German, "Do you know a women by the name of Barbara Zigmund?" She looks at me strangely and replies, "Yes, I am Barbara Zigmund, and who are you?"

I respond in Yiddish, saying, "Mama, don't you *recognize* me?"

I don't know why, but I suddenly start to reach for the cookies and try to take the teakettle from her hand. She stops me and tells me to go outside and wait for her; she will take care of everything.

While waiting for my mother outside, I begin to wonder why neither one of us recognized the other. I realize that, in her case, the answer is quite simple: in spite of the miserable conditions in the concentration camp, I've grown several centimeters and my face has begun to change into the face of a man. Now I am *taller* than my mother; when we last saw each other two and a half years ago I was *shorter* than she is. The reason I didn't recognize *her* must be nervousness and her white nurse's uniform, because I *did* recognize her when she walked down the road beside me and other prisoners last year.

When she returns, she tells me this is an old folks' home. The tea and cookies I saw were for a German couple who came to pick up their father and take him west. At first she thought I was their chauffeur.

Now, she explains, she is taking me to another convent in the same town where my Aunt Sarah is working as an Aryan. That convent has a farm, a stable for cows and a barn—and also a summer and a winter residence. In the winter, she explains, the summer residence is unoccupied. This is where my Aunt Sarah will keep me hidden until the war ends.

Now I Must Live
With My Guilt

Three days after I arrive, my mother brings two more prisoners who escaped from the march for Aunt Sarah to hide. These are the people my father used as middlemen to contact my mother. It is from them that Mother and I learn that my father died on the death march on the way to the Gross Rosen concentration camp.

Now I am tortured by feelings of guilt. I say to myself, "You were able to help your cousin Janek escape. Why didn't you grab your father when you ran from the death march?"

I don't know if I'll ever understand why I acted the way I did. When I relive the exact moment when I knew we must escape or be killed, I don't see how I could have acted differently. It was just a split second; there was no time to weigh the pros and cons. I *did* tell my father that I was leaving. Why didn't he follow me? Now I may never know. Perhaps his prayer for my grandfather was the most important thing to him at the time. Perhaps he didn't hear me. Perhaps he believed that God would save us. Will I ever know?

And what about *me*? Maybe I realized—at the moment I ran—that it's okay to play Russian roulette with your own life, but it's irresponsible to do it with anyone else's life. Maybe I just didn't try hard enough to bring my father with me because this was what I was thinking. Am I lying to myself?

Aunt Sarah has taken enormous risks in hiding and caring for three escaped Jews under very difficult circumstances. She works as a farmhand in this convent and is taking care of her niece Ruzia, the older daughter of Uncle Moses. Aunt Sarah must be extremely careful that other farm hands don't discover what she's up to.

Because we're hiding in a summer residence, there is no running water in the winter. We must use a metal bucket as a toilet, and Aunt Sarah must empty it every morning and mix its contents in with the cow manure in the stable. Fortunately, she starts her work shift at 4:00 a.m. when no one is around to see her switching buckets.

Aunt Sarah is wonderful. When she milks the cows, she brings us fresh milk, and after she boils potatoes for the pigs and goes to the henhouse, she brings us piping hot potatoes and hard boiled eggs.

It's the beginning of March and we're still here. Back in January we had hoped that it would take just a few days for the Russians to cross the Oder and Neisse rivers and free us. Instead, they halted their offensive until now and we have been hiding in the summer residence for six weeks. During all this time, we have had no chance to take a bath, and hundreds of lice have nested on our bodies. They drive us crazy with itching, especially at night, and they keep us busy every day on our own personal search-and-destroy missions. But no matter how many of them we find and kill, there are always more to take their place.

At last the Russians have started a very intensive artillery attack on the entire region around here. During the bombing of an anti-aircraft battery that the Germans operate behind the convent, the Germans come to close the shutters on all the windows in the summer residence. We manage to get out without them seeing us, but it's a close call. Afterward, Aunt Sarah has us leave the summer residence and go into the barn, one at a time.

"When you all get there," she says, "find a spot in the loft. I will be in touch with you and take care of everything."

We slip out of the summer residence separately and meet in the barn, where we find a spot to hide under the rafters of the tiled roof. We are worried about Aunt Sarah, who is under terrible stress.

"Don't worry," we tell her. "If we get caught, we'll say that we escaped from the march and broke into this barn."

Things go quite well until one day the Russian planes start strafing the tiles off the roof above us. We are in such danger that we have to run down to the lower barn. That's when we are discovered by one of the convent's other workers, who happens to speak Polish.

We give him the prepared story that we had escaped and broken into the barn. Then he calls Aunt Sarah in to help him decide what to do. When she comes, she acts very surprised to see these three Jewish people and suggests that we hide in one of the abandoned German homes. She even offers to take us there. We accept her offer and thank them both.

When we are a safe distance away, Aunt Sarah tells us that she is taking us to an abandoned house across the street from the convent where my mother works. She tells us how glad she is that her co-worker didn't question our story or suspect her involvement with us.

After we thank her for all the hard work and risks she took to save our lives, I climb in an unlocked window on the side of the house and open the main entrance door for my friends. Inside, the house is sparkling clean.

The first things we look for in the kitchen are food and water. We even manage to get the water heater going after several tries. That means that we can finally take baths.

That makes us get the giggles. One of us says, "You mean to tell me that you're going to put on the same clothing over the same lice? We must find some Lysol to disinfect ourselves–and a change of clothing."

What we can't find in "our" house we look for in other houses in the neighborhood until we find what we need. Of course, we have to keep a low profile in order not to get caught, but the place is really like a ghost town, totally abandoned with the exception of the old people in the convent where my mother works.

Once, Mother comes to check on us, and I tell her, "Don't worry about us. We will take good care of ourselves."

Then she tells us that the priest will be conducting a prayer service and mass in the basement of the convent: we can go and pretend to be Catholic and participate in the service. I promise that I will come as a good Catholic to pray at her convent. When she leaves, she has a big smile on her face.

Getting rid of the old clothing is simple enough, but getting rid of the lice on our bodies is a lot more difficult. I remember that lice were one of the ten plagues visited upon the Egyptians, yet I never thought of them as a big deal until I had them myself. Now that we have a chance to get clean, we have to shave off every bit of hair we have on any part of our body and clean everything with Lysol, but even that isn't enough. They are imbedded in our skin, so it takes quite a while, many hot baths, many bottles of Lysol and the burning skin it produces to finally get rid of them.

In picking the clothing we should wear, we have to be careful not to look like Germans. Rather, we choose things that make us look like the people of Poland, and that is fine with us because we speak Polish.

We never go outside together; instead, we decide where to go and then walk there one by one so as not to raise suspicions. We have to go to different homes to replenish our food supplies. Fortunately it is cold outside and the food doesn't spoil.

It is quite boring to hang around our hiding place all day, so I decide to go to the convent and volunteer to help out with certain chores. Of course, no one has any inkling that my mother and I are related. While I am working there, I am given cooked meals.

I even decide to go to Mass, which is a strange experience. Here I am in the basement of the convent with a bunch of elderly people—some seated in chairs, others in wheel chairs with nurses at their sides, all listening to the priest while artillery shells explode.

At one point, the priest is saying something in Latin as he comes around and places a small wafer on the tongue of each worshiper. My first thought is, *Is it Kosher for me to accept this wafer?* Then I think to myself, *You'd better accept it if you don't want to raise any suspicions.* And one more thought pops up into my mind: *What would my father do if he saw his son participating in a Catholic mass?* But I also realize that a Jew is always allowed to ignore certain religious teachings for the sake of survival.

When I leave the convent to return to the abandoned home where we live, I am met with a barrage of artillery fire. Shells are falling and exploding all over the place, and the air is filled with the sound of Russian planes diving to bomb German ground targets. For a minute I consider returning to the convent basement, where it would be a lot safer, but instead I decide to make a run for it. Fortunately I am not hit by the artillery fire or flying debris.

At the house the guys are overjoyed by the air attacks. They have opened a bottle of Schnapps to celebrate our liberation, which they are sure will happen any time now. The Schnapps helps us get a good night's sleep, and–sure enough–in the morning we are awakened by someone pounding on the door. When we open it, there are several Russian soldiers outside, demanding to know who we are.

We answer them in Polish and show them the tattooed numbers on our arms. Then their attitudes changes completely, and they tell us that we can start our journey home whenever we wish. At that, all of us jump up and down for joy, hugging and thanking the Russian soldiers. It is the end of March 1945.

I immediately run to meet my mother at the convent. Finally, we are able to hug each other openly, without any fear. It is natural and genuine! I have longed for this hug for over two and a half years. Now my emotions get the best of me and I cry like a baby. It feels good to finally let go and express the pain I feel–and accept my mother's love.

Making Our Way Back Home

We've decided to waste no time in leaving. We have no idea *how* we'll get home. We've just decided to take the most essential items and get right on the road going east towards Poland. We figure that we can spend the nights in abandoned German homes until we get there.

I've already packed my few items and am just waiting for Mother to pack hers. It seems to be taking a long time.

Oh my God! Here she comes, dragging two huge, overstuffed bags down the stairs. "Mother," I say, "These bags will just weigh us down and we won't be able to walk with them. We do not need all of this. All we need is to get to Jaworzno as soon as possible!" I think she's going to challenge me, but she quickly relents. We are able to throw away most of the stuff, and soon we're on our way, walking towards the main highway.

On the highway, nothing has changed except there is no death march. The road is clogged with Russian military vehicles, ranging from horse-drawn sleds to heavy tanks. There are also many German civilians. While most of the military traffic is going west, some military vehicles are traveling in the same direction we are and we hope to hitch a ride on one of them.

We've been walking for several hours and have tried to flag down several military vehicles, but so far no luck.

Oh, I spoke too soon. Now a truck with two soldiers in the cab is stopping for us. They ask Mother to sit up in front with them and tell me to climb into the truck bed.

At last we are on our way. I can just picture our arrival in Jaworzno. Maybe my brother will come home, too. Maybe other members of our family survived the war.

We've been riding for quite awhile now, so I'll peek into the cab and see how Mother is doing. But what I see is that something is wrong. The driver and my mother, who is on the right side of the cab, seem to be fighting.

I immediately knock on the back window and ask the driver to stop the truck. When he stops, I climb to the other side of the truck bed and open the door so that Mother can get out, but the driver is holding onto her hand and won't let go.

I run around to the driver's side and plead with him to let her go. The next thing I know, he swings the door open and pulls out a machine gun, which he aims straight at me. I jump into the ditch beside the road and immediately feel a sharp, searing pain. I can't see the driver and he can't see me, but I can hear the other soldier trying to calm him down. I wait a minute and then I hear the truck drive away.

At first I fear that Mother is still in it, but then I hear her voice.

"I'm over here, Mother," I call out. But when she peers over the edge of the ditch, I am still lying on the ground.

"What happened, Mother?" I ask.

"I'll tell you all that later," she replies. "Right now we'd better get going. It's getting late."

I try to struggle to my feet, but I can't.

"I'm not able to move my left leg," I tell her. "I can't walk!"

"All right," she says, "stay there while I go for help."

I don't want to be parted from her for even a few minutes, and this might take hours, but there is no alternative. I can't move an inch, much less walk all the way back to Jaworzno.

I don't know how long Mother has been gone, but it's beginning to get dark and I'm starting to be worried. And then suddenly she appears at the edge of the ditch.

"I had to go to one of the abandoned houses to find a baby carriage so I could wheel you the rest of the way," she says in her matter-of-fact manner. "Oh, and I've brought some towels with me. We'll wrap them around your leg so you won't move it and hurt yourself even more. Now let's get you out of that ditch!"

Well, that is definitely easier said than done. I have to slide out of the ditch backwards on my rear end!

Once I am out of the ditch, Mother helps me get up on my feet and into the baby carriage. Me in a baby carriage? Am I ever glad that no one I know can see us!

By now it's quite dark, so Mother wheels me to an abandoned home off the road where we can spend the night. While we're here, Mother tries both hot and cold compresses on my leg to see which one makes me feel more comfortable. I tell her that the ice seems to temporarily reduce the pain.

Once I'm settled, she wanders around the house to find the ingredients for my first home-cooked meal in nearly three years. I don't know how she managed, but the food tastes heavenly. Then she tells me what happened to her in the cab of that military vehicle.

She explains that the Russian driver was drunk and tried to make a pass at her. The only reason she got away was that the other soldier intervened and she was able to open the door and jump out when the driver wasn't looking. And then she says that because he was drunk, he could not be held responsible for his actions. According to her, "These soldiers are away from their families for months fighting a cruel war,

108

and they try to drown their sorrows in vodka. This is the result of it." I have my leg as a painful reminder of this incident, and I'm not quite so forgiving, though I recall having thoughts similar to Mother's when the English prisoner of war tried to rape me.

For the rest of the evening, we talk about how many of our family members will return to Jaworzno and how we are going to reestablish our roots and settle there. I tell her that Jaworzno—and for that matter all of Poland—is so drenched with Jewish blood it is unlikely that any of us would be happy staying there.

"And if we have to start anew," I say, "we should do it in the Promised Land. That is where our ancestors came from and that is where we have to return. We've had enough of persecution and humiliation. It's time to stand up for ourselves!"

My mother has never heard me state my feelings so strongly. She doesn't realize how violated I feel by all the horrors I experienced in the last few years and, most of all, how much I hated the submissiveness of the Jewish masses going like sheep to the slaughterhouse.

After I share my feelings with Mother, I feel better. I even get a good night's sleep in spite of the pain in my leg every time I turn over.

We get up in the morning, have a quick breakfast and are ready to move on. I'm so embarrassed that my mother has to wheel me around like a baby, but I have no choice. I'm sure that in time my leg will heal itself.

The distance from here to Jaworzno is about 120 kilometers (or 75 miles), which is a long distance to wheel a 15-year-old in a baby carriage. Mother decides that once we reach the town of Gleiwitz, she will wheel me straight into the Russian commander's office and ask him to provide us with some mode of transportation. My mother's determination is not something to mess with. She has the strength of a lioness and the endurance of a tiger. This is what got her on the snow-covered roads to the Blechhammer concentration camp to find my father and me. The fact that I am alive to ride in this baby carriage is the payoff of that determination.

It takes most of the day for us to get to Gleiwitz, so Mother decides that it is best to meet the local military commander in the early morning rather than this evening. We spend the night in another abandoned home, but it contains no food for us. Fortunately Mother has saved a substantial amount of German money, so she is able to buy a few things.

Morning comes all too soon, and we must be on our way. But before we go to the Russian commander, Mother wants us to see a doctor. Because she speaks German so well, it isn't long before she finds one. He says that I have a severe muscular inflammation in my leg and suggests that we heat some sand bags in the oven and then use them as a compress. He tells me to exercise by doing knee bends in a lying position and in six weeks I'll be able to do everything. Easy for him to say!

Next we find out where the Russian commander has his office, and we head there, Mother striding along wheeling her "baby." When we get into the commander's office, we see a rather unattractive man with a big, hooked nose. He turns the charm on and says to my mother, "What is a beautiful woman like you doing in this godforsaken place?"

Mother smiles at him and says in Yiddish, "You think if I had a choice I would be here?"

He looks at her and says, in all innocence, "What makes you think that I understand Yiddish?"

My mother replies, "With a nose like that what else could you be but Jewish?"

He laughs and says, "Nose? So what can I do for you in plain Yiddish."

She tells him our story and he arranges for us to get a ride to Katowice, which is about 24 kilometers (15 miles) from Jaworzno. "From there," he says, "you can take a regular bus to Jaworzno." He also arranges for Mother to exchange her deutsche marks for zlotys, the

Polish money used in Katowice. Mother thanks him for his generous help and we are on our way.

When we arrive, we learn that there is no regular bus service going to Jaworzno yet—just horse-drawn carriages and trucks that carry supplies between the two cities. The distance is short, so Mother arranges for us to ride on a freight truck later that day. But first she wants to contact members of the Jewish community here in Katowice to find out what kind of help is available to Jewish survivors under Poland's new communist regime.

What she hears is not promising. A man at the Jewish Community Association of Katowice tells her point-blank, "You will not be able to go into your own home if it is occupied by a Polish family. You will not be able to retrieve any of your possessions that are used by a Polish family. If you have something hidden or buried in your house, you will not be able to claim it without the permission of the present occupants. The best the Polish town hall will do for you is find you a place to stay with other Jewish survivors in Jewish homes that are unoccupied or abandoned. Forewarned is forearmed."

After we leave the Jewish Community Association office, Mother wheels me to the spot where truck drivers pick up passengers and earn a little extra money in the process.

We wait for over half an hour for a truck that can take us, until finally a driver stops and yells, *"do Jaworzna"* (to Jaworzno). Mother goes over to him and points to me while they settle on a price. I have to be helped up into the cab while the driver loads the baby carriage into the back. Then we are on our way.

My mother and the driver carry on a lively conversation. She asks him many questions about what is going on in Jaworzno and who is in charge of the town hall. She also asks if there are any Jews who have returned to Jaworzno and where they live.

The driver says that everything is controlled by the local Communist Party. He suggests that he drop us off at the town hall, where Mother can get more information.

111

My beloved grandfather's house as it appeared in 2000, marred by peeling paint and graffiti

Before long, the landmark chimneys of the Jaworzno coal mines come into view in the distance, and we know we are home. We ask the driver to turn into Mickiewicza Street so we can take a peek at our house before we get off at the town hall. As we pass the school and our house, my heart skips a beat.

Mother asks the driver to stop for a moment so we can see if there is any sign of life in our house, but we change our minds and go straight to the town hall. Mother pays the driver and thanks him. Then she asks him to help me get off the truck and put me in the baby carriage while she goes into the town hall to make arrangements so that we can get a roof over our heads.

Inside, she finds out that Aunt Sarah and Ruzia are already in town and have requested that we be housed with them. She is given an address that was the old Laufer home, located behind the church.

Mother wheels me across the *Rynek* (Marketplace) past my grandfather's house to the Laufers' place. Passing by my grandfather's house, we see that the pharmacy is still located there, but the stationery store that grandfather owned has been replaced by a hardware store. The house is now occupied by a bunch of drunken tramps who are supported and supervised by the town's social services department. We are not allowed to go there.

When we get to the Laufer home, we are greeted by Aunt Sarah, Ruzia and a survivor from the Laufer family. It's a big house with plenty of room for all of us. We give Aunt Sarah the sordid details of our trip to Jaworzno and settle in for the night.

This morning Mother wants to take me to our old family doctor so he can look at my leg. Oddly enough he comes up with the same diagnosis as the other doctor and prescribes the same remedy: burlap sacks filled with sand. The only difference is that he tells me to keep my leg elevated.

The First Leg of My Journey to the Promised Land

Now there's nothing to do but wait for family members to come back home. Nights are spent sitting wondering if any of our loved ones have survived. Every time someone knocks on the door, we hope that it is one of our close relatives, and every time we are disappointed. It has been very difficult for us.

It has been especially hard for me because of the guilt feelings I have for leaving my father behind. These feelings keep cropping up even though it would have been virtually impossible for the two of us to escape together at that particular moment. But the worst of it is that Mother brought the subject up during one of our conversations. "How could you possibly have escaped without taking your father with you?" she asked.

The minute the words were out of her mouth, I burst into tears. While I deeply love my mother and understand her feelings, I wish she had left her question unasked.

Then, in the middle of my despair, we learned that my brother Moses David did not survive the war. In our immediate family, only my mother and I survived.

These thoughts occupy my mind all the time, but in the mean while we must have food on the table, and I feel I must help. Aunt Sarah is very familiar with the cities of Krakow and Katowice and she's very shrewd about bargaining, so she has decided to get involved in the black market trade between the two cities. Now that my injured leg has started to heal, I tag along with her. While I learn the tricks of the trade in those cities, I can help her by carrying goods from one place to another, and with both of us working we can make more money for food.

With the end of the war in Europe, a lot more trading is going on. Now we're dealing in the currencies of the allied countries and Russia and Eastern Europe. There's also a huge demand for the US dollar and American cigarettes, so the black market is thriving and we are able to earn a living. That's the good news.

The bad news is that I don't like the way we're living. There seems to be no meaning to our lives, and I feel as if mine is being wasted. We Jews just accept things as they are and do nothing to change them. Adding to my frustration is the fact that the small towns in Poland are now under the command of the Communist Party faithful. Under their "leadership" there is a great deal of corruption and mismanagement. They resent the fact that we Jewish survivors want our homes back. Actually, they hate Jews but they don't say so openly. Instead, they say, "Oh, it would not be right for you to displace the people who are living in your homes just because you survived the concentration camps. Oh no, they can't be asked to pay you for your property. That would be wrong." So after years of Nazi persecution, this is what we have to put up with.

Well I am not willing to accept rejection and discrimination. I don't think that as a Jew I'm inferior to other people. And so my mind is turning more and more often to the only remedy I can think of: we Jews must go to the Promised Land and establish our own independent state.

Perhaps no experience is wasted in this life of ours. During one of my trips to Krakow with Aunt Sarah, I met a young boy by the name of Lolek Halperin. Lolek survived the war while being sheltered in an orphanage in Budapest, Hungary. The orphanage is run by a Dr.

115

Kotarba, who received the funding for it from the Zionists. After the war ended, Lolek traveled from Budapest to Krakow to see if any of his relatives had survived, but unfortunately none of them had. Soon he returned to the orphanage.

As Lolek and I got better acquainted, he explained to me in detail the activities and goals of the Zionist organization. The main goal is to settle Jews in Palestine and create an independent national home for them so as to end, once and for all, the persecution and discrimination our people have suffered for centuries.

When Lolek told me all this, I got very excited about the possibility of reclaiming our historical rights in the land of our patriarchs: Abraham, Isaac and Jacob. All this talk about Zionism re-ignited in me the spark that Uncle Moses had planted at the beginning of the war. I was so excited I told Lolek that I wanted to leave Poland and go with him to Budapest next week.

Before we parted, we set a date and time to meet at the Krakow railroad station so we could take the train together. And then came the hard part: when I returned to Jaworzno, I told my mother of my decision. She tried very hard to get me to change my mind, but after a lengthy and painful discussion I told her that my decision was final. "I have a sacred obligation to the memory of our lost family members and to the cause of Jews everywhere," I told her. After that, she reluctantly accepted my decision and said that she would go to the train station with me.

That hasn't made it easy to just pick up and go. Oh, I'm glad that I've taken a step in shaping my own destiny. It's something I feel very strongly about, and I would never be at peace with myself if I didn't do it. But leaving my mother and our few remaining family members has been one of the most painful things I've ever done.

I had a tearful parting with my Aunt Sarah and cousin Ruzia. As Mother and I boarded the bus to Krakow, I was leaving with a heavy heart as I remembered all the things my aunt had done for me. But the worst hurdle for me to overcome would be saying goodbye to Mother at the train station.

On the station platform, Lolek is waiting for me at the exact spot we agreed on. I introduce him to my mother, and almost immediately the call comes —"All Aboard!" Quickly, I hug my mother and start to say goodbye, but she clings to me and starts to cry. "Don't leave me, don't abandon me!" I try to comfort her, but what can I say that will make her understand how important it is for me to go? As I hear the final "All Aboard!" I suddenly say, "Look Mom, maybe you could afford to lose a husband and three children, but I don't want that to happen to me! I must do something about it!"

As soon as the words are out of my mouth, I realize how cruel they sound to her and how bad she must feel. But it's too late to take them back. The doors to the train cars are being slammed shut, and Lolek and I have to run to get on board.

As the train pulls away, I see my mother standing on the platform weeping, and my heart sinks. I deeply regret having spoken to her so bluntly, but my feelings are raw, my reality is cruel and that is all I could think to blurt out at the time.

Now, too late, I remember what Mother always used to say to me: "You are always in possession of the word you have not uttered, but once it is said, it is in the public domain." There are times I hate myself, and this is one of them.

The train is loaded to the hilt with passengers. We're lucky to have squeezed into two seats. Suddenly, two Russian soldiers enter our car and begin robbing passengers of their valuables. They are mostly interested in wristwatches and gold rings. Shortly after they leave, more soldiers come to do the same thing. It's total anarchy, but no one can do anything about it.

The train makes a long stop in Vienna, Austria, but Lolek and I don't dare go out and into the station because we know we would never get our seats back. At least we have food—sandwiches and cookies Mother prepared for us and tea with lemon.

The trip from Vienna to Budapest has taken several hours, but it has been several hours of spectacular scenery. The Danube River and the mountains are breathtakingly beautiful.

Now a new set of Russian thieves is here, but their tactics are the same. When they approach us, we tell them that we already donated our watches on the first leg of the trip.

After they leave, Lolek briefs me on the educational program in the orphanage where we will live. It is a very rich curriculum, ranging from Hebrew language and Jewish history to math and science to folk dances. Having missed two and a half years of schooling, I find it very exciting—and a bit frightening. I hope my lack of schooling won't pose any problems for me. Well, nothing to do but find out.

As the train pulls into the Budapest railroad station, we get off and catch a bus to the orphanage. Lolek has been in this city for quite a while, so he knows his way around *and* he speaks Hungarian.

"Look," he says as the bus pulls away, "the city is divided in two by the Danube River, into Buda and Pest. They are connected by beautiful bridges."

He's right. It really is a lovely city.

When we arrive at the orphanage, we discover that all the children are out at a summer camp in the mountains. The caretaker tells Lolek that Dr. Kotarba left railway tickets and instructions that we are to join the group there. But first, we will stay overnight at the orphanage.

After a good night's sleep, Lolek and I are ready to be on our way. The caretaker has lived up to his title: he has fed us well, and now he's prepared sandwiches for us to take on our trip to the mountains.

Here in Hungary, the trains are clean and on schedule. Today's trip is another beautiful one that passes through mountains and lakes all the way to our destination, a place called Silwashvarot.

Here, we have to take a horse-drawn wagon from the railroad station to our group's camping site, and what a site it is! In the middle is a large rectangular lawn where the boys and girls are playing volleyball and soccer. At one end of the lawn is a very large tent with tables and benches. It is used as a dining room. Lining either side of the grass are tents where the children sleep. Lolek introduces me to Dr. Kotarba and some of the teachers, who urge me to make myself comfortable. But I can't tear my eyes away from the scene of kids playing happily, free from any worries. As I keep watching, I realize that these youngsters probably never had to go through the ordeals that I was subjected to for the past two and a half years. When I ask Lolek about them, he says that there are some Hungarians, but the majority are Polish Jews who lost their parents in the Holocaust.

Before dinner, Lolek and I are assigned to the same tent and get ready to join the group for their meal. At dinner, I learn that the language spoken by most of the children is Polish, although those who have been in Hungary long enough are able to communicate with the local children in Hungarian.

After dinner all of us gather around a bonfire and begin singing Hebrew songs, Yiddish songs, Russian songs—even some Polish songs. Some of the kids are dancing Jewish dances, the polka and other folk dances. Everyone, including me, is having a great time. I am very excited by this new experience. I just hope that I will be able to adjust without any problems. Tonight, anyway, the kids are eager to teach me the songs and dances.

My 10 days at the summer camp have flown by, and now it's time for all of us to take the train back to Budapest and start school. Lolek warns me that I will find our course of study to be both rich and demanding—rich because of the variety of subjects we study in great detail and demanding because of the self-discipline expected of us. Well, I don't think I'll mind the discipline, because it might make me gain real self-respect. There's a creative energy in this group that makes itself felt in everything we do.

School has been in session for a few weeks now, and I must say that it certainly has posed an enormous challenge for me. Not having any formal schooling for so long means that I have to attend classes with youngsters who are as much as three years younger than me. That certainly doesn't do anything for my self-esteem! I may be way beyond these kids in life experiences, but I have to buckle down and study hard to try to catch up with them in my classes. Thank God they are giving me tutoring and extra reading materials to help me bridge the gap, but I still have trouble because I'm so impatient. It's not just embarrassing for a 16-year-old to be in a classroom with 13-year-olds; I'm upset with *myself* a lot of the time for not making faster progress. Feeling awkward and out of place is *not* my cup of tea. There's an old saying, *What brains can't accomplish, time always will,* but try telling this to a hotheaded 16-year-old *Meshugener* (crazy) boy.

I'm Chosen for a
Very Important Mission

I'm starting to learn a hard fact of life: the standard of living and civil liberties for Jewish survivors of the war are far better in the Western occupied zone of Europe (West Germany, France, Belgium, The Netherlands Britain etc.) than in the Russian-occupied zone (East Germany, Poland, Hungary, Czechoslovakia and the Balkan countries). In the Western zone, Jewish survivors of the Nazi concentration camps are organized by different political Zionist organizations for the purpose of resettling in Palestine. Various Jewish organizations in the United States are sending money that allows the Zionist movement to buy parched tracts of land from Palestinians all over the Holy Land and convert them into beautiful farmland. They literally grow the most amazing crops right in the middle of the desert!

For a long time, the British ruled Palestine and refused to let Jews settle there, but now we are determined to reclaim our homeland. But for us here at the orphanage, there's a problem: in the Russian zone, where we now live, Zionism is outlawed. For this reason, Dr. Kotarba, with the consent of the Zionist organization *Hashomer Hatzair* (The Young Guardian), has decided that we must relocate into the American zone in West Germany.

This of course poses many logistical and legal problems for us. For one thing, it is forbidden to cross from the Russian to the American zone. So how is the good doctor going to smuggle all 70 of us across the border without being caught? It's going to take some careful planning and coordinated help from all the Zionist organizations. And here's another problem: the ages of the children in the orphanage range from 2 to 17, making the move all the more difficult.

Just when I was beginning to wonder if Dr. Kotarba would ever find a solution, he and the Zionist organization have decided to send three of the more mature kids on a fact-finding mission to Bratislava in Czechoslovakia. And guess what? The three chosen for that task are Zwiczka, Lolek and me!

This is a very big responsibility. Our task is to insure that there are facilities in Bratislava large enough to house our group for a short time. Everyone in the orphanage must leave by tour bus no later than the tenth of December. When we get to Bratislava, we will stay there for a few nights in the facility that Zwiczka, Lolek and I choose. Then no later than the twentieth of December, we will travel on to Prague and stay there until we can cross the border into West Germany. We have to do all of this as tourists, without raising any suspicion on the part of the authorities.

Preparations for our fact-finding trip will be made by the central Zionist organization, but then we'll be on our own—three teenaged boys in charge of planning a safe journey for 70 orphans! It's a huge responsibility, and you can imagine how proud I am to have been picked to help carry it out.

We left by train this morning. In Bratislava we were met by the representative of the Zionist team. Luckily, Zwiczka was born here and is fluent in the language, so he has been very helpful in communicating our needs to the locals.

The place we've chosen for the children to stay in Bratislava is not nearly as nice as the orphanage, but we figure that it will be good for our group to sacrifice some creature comforts in order to reach our goal.

After spending two hectic days in Bratislava, we have finished making all the arrangements and are returning to Budapest on the train, which (surprise, surprise) is filled with Russian soldiers stealing whatever they can from the passengers. Fortunately, our group of 70 will be traveling by bus, so they will be spared that experience.

We can hardly wait to tell Dr. Kotarba about the facilities we visited in Bratislava and everything we saw there. Now it's up to him and the Zionist organization to make final arrangements for the trip.

It's only three days later, and Dr. Kotarba has notified us that the trip will take place next Sunday morning. Everyone is being told to take only a few personal items and be ready to leave by 6:00 a.m. sharp.

On Saturday evening we celebrated our departure by singing Hebrew and Yiddish songs and dancing all sorts of folk dances. We were so excited because we knew that today we would be one step closer to the Promised Land.

It's very early on Sunday morning, and the children are all ready and anxious to get into the two buses that are waiting outside. But first, we all stand at attention and sing the Hebrew national anthem. As the bus doors swing open, the kitchen staff hands us sandwiches and wishes us well. And then we're on our way.

If we are stopped by the authorities, they will have had no trouble believing that this group of kids is just on an outing, because all of us are singing and having a great time. One of the songs is *"Am Israel Chai, Chai vekayam"* (The Jewish people are Alive, Alive and Determined).

As we sing, I am thinking a great deal about the significance of that song for us. Here I am among a group of children who survived a Holocaust where 6 million Jews were brutally exterminated by the Nazis, and I can't help but wonder, *What is it that we have going for us that allows us to carry on after 2,000 years of exile from our homeland, 2,000 years of persecution?*

The more I think about this question, the more I believe I know the answer. For 40 years the Jews lived in exile in Egypt, and then they were led out of Egyptian slavery by Moses. From Moses, they received the Ten Commandments, the world's first-known moral code. This was later expanded into our holy book, the Torah, which was enriched by other writings during our people's 20 centuries of exile in Christian and Muslim lands. It was our religious and moral and ethical convictions that kept us strong.

The Jews of biblical times were known as a stubborn people, and I guess that's a good thing to be. So were we able to survive for 2,000 years because we were constantly harassed and persecuted, or was it because of our ethical and moral traditions?

Well, I think the answer is *both*. Every year during Passover we celebrate the Exodus from Egyptian slavery. Every year, we recite *Leshana Habaa Bejerushalayim* (Next year we hope to celebrate in Jerusalem). I believe that this tradition has kept the yearning and desire to return to our homeland alive for all those centuries.

While all of these facts of Jewish history are running through my mind, the buses are making their way into Bratislava, where we are welcomed by Zionist representatives. No sooner are we off the buses than they give us great news—Friday morning we will leave for Prague!

The few days we have spent in Bratislava have gone by quickly, and we have learned so much about the Promised Land. We have heard lectures by members of the Zionist Pioneers movement—young people who live on a kibbutz, or commune. They have told us what life and work are like there and how, with new agricultural methods and irrigation, they can grow amazing crops in the desert. Some day soon, we will be on a kibbutz, too.

On Thursday evening we all gathered around a bonfire to celebrate our last night in Bratislava, and the young kibbutz members taught us new folk dances and songs. On Friday morning the buses arrived on schedule. We boarded them quickly and were soon on our way to Prague.

By the time we arrived, it was already pitch dark outside. As soon as we were assigned our rooms in what during the war was a military compound, we rushed into the mess hall to get our evening meal. There, we met children belonging to many different Zionist organizations, all waiting to cross into the Western zone.

Our Midnight Walk
Across the Border

It's the Christmas season, 1945, and the adults think that this might be a good time for us to sneak across the border—while the Christians are busy with their celebrations. The Zionist organizations that are helping us have this smuggling routine worked out to the last detail, so everything should go like clockwork.

It's New Year's Eve, and we've been in Prague for two weeks, but we've just learned that tonight's the night. We will be bused to a place near the border late this evening, and from there we will have to walk in complete silence in deep snows for about 4 kilometers (2½miles). They told us that the crossing should take less than an hour from start to finish.

The Zionists have taught us how to take care of the small children. We will carry them across the snow in the forest, and we must do so in absolute silence. It's scary, but we are all excited as we bundle up and get in line for the bus ride.

The buses take us to a dimly lighted village, where we line up again. One of the villagers leads us into the forest, where the shadows of the trees mingle with the moving shadows of our bodies on the snow. It's creepy, but once we get used to the shadows moving on the surface of

126

the snow, we begin to relax. It's a beautiful starlit night with lights flickering in the distance.

The walk has gone quite well, but suddenly our Russian amputee discovers one of the little children in the deep snow when he sets down one of his crutches. He looks down at the little fellow and says, "Kitchie, Kitchie," and we have a hard time keeping everyone quiet. We realize that the little boy has fallen, and we might have left him behind if the amputee hadn't found him. So we stop and count noses to be sure that everyone is still with us.

It's only taken a little more than an hour for us to reach a village on the American side of the border, and here we find two buses waiting to take us to our new location in Ansbach, West Germany. Once the buses start moving, we all burst out singing various Hebrew songs.

We arrive at Ansbach at the crack of dawn. Many of us have been dozing, but now we wake to see a cluster of medieval stone buildings. This place where we will stay is a former German officers' training school, and it's immense!

Once we get settled, we learn that there are about a half dozen Zionist organizations in these facilities, with about 600 children of various ages. We also learn that there is fierce competition among these organizations in all kinds of sports.

Just as in Bratislava and Prague, we are to be given intensive lessons in Hebrew, the history and accomplishments of the pioneers in Palestine and the importance of defending our national home. That's in addition to the normal classes in math, science and literature.

Intense—you'd better believe it! We are kept busy from the wee hours of the morning until late at night. There are many lectures on land reclamation, irrigation and maximizing the productivity of the land. In addition, there are special training classes that teach us various techniques of self-defense. It's sobering to realize that we will be fighting like soldiers once we get to the Promised Land.

One thing that makes me really happy is that I have caught up with my classmates in all my studies. This certainly makes me feel a lot more comfortable than I was in the beginning and puts me in a relaxed mood.

We're Almost on Our Way to Palestine

Many months have passed, but through all of the good times I've had since I left my mother, I have been unable to forgive myself for the cruel things I said to her at the train station in Krakow. I cannot leave for Palestine without making amends.

This is easier said than done, because as it turns out she is no longer in Jaworzno, and I have no idea where she has gone. Finally, I am advised to contact the United Nations Relief Agency, and thank God they are able to locate her. Today she is living in Zeilsheim, which is near Frankfurt in West Germany.

I know that I must find her and apologize for my thoughtless remarks before I go to Palestine. Otherwise, I may never have a chance. But what can I say? I've thought so much about this, going back in my mind to that day in Krakow and trying to figure out exactly what I did wrong or what I could have done differently. I've decided that it was not so much *what* I said that hurt her, it was the *way* I said it. I am not less convinced of my argument now than I was then, but in the meantime I've learned a few things and matured a little. That surely helps.

Not feeling that I can come up with the right approach on my own, I decide to talk to some of my teachers and counselors. I give them a detailed description of what happened at the Krakow station, along with the story of how Mother and I survived the war. I tell them how remorseful I am about the harsh words I used and the pain I inflicted on her.

What they do is very useful: they make me put myself in my mother's place. How, they ask, would you have felt at the time if you had been in her shoes? How would you feel about everything now? Once we talk about this, they give me helpful suggestions about how to conduct myself in conversations with Mother.

I decide not to warn Mother that I am coming. I want it to be a surprise. So I take the railroad to Frankfurt and from there I take a bus to Zeilsheim. I have a bit of trouble locating the place, but I finally find it. I am about to press the buzzer, but I hesitate, wondering what kind of reception I will get.

When I screw up my courage and ring the buzzer, my Aunt Sarah comes to the door and yells out at top of her voice, "Shmilek is here!" Mother comes running to the door and gives me a huge hug, as tears of joy run down her cheeks. I have grown a lot since we parted, and she is very happy to see me.

I spend several days with my mother and the rest of the family in Zeilsheim. Mother and I have calm and productive discussions about our differences. I apologize to her for my harsh behavior at the Krakow station–apologies she gracefully accepts. We reach a point of mutual understanding and respect for each other's viewpoints, and I promise that I will write to her and the family.

I also assure her that I will keep the traditions of the family, even though I am not a religious or orthodox Jew. I tell her that I'll always be faithful to the Silberberg code of ethics, honesty and decency. As I leave for Ansbach, I am deeply satisfied that I have contacted Mother and established a new, loving relationship with her. The visit with her helps me get a load off my chest and frees some energy that I will need for the difficult tasks ahead.

My reunion with my mother in the summer of 1946. Mother is on the left; Ruzia and Aunt Sarah are on the right.

More months have passed, and everyone here is waiting impatiently for our turn to leave Germany for one of the Mediterranean harbors where we can board a ship to take us to Palestine. But trying to reach the Promised Land, it turns out, is very complicated. The British, who actually govern Palestine, are loyal to the Arab oil sheikdoms in the Middle East, and they don't want to resettle the Jews in Palestine. So the British use their vast fleet of ships to prevent Jewish immigrants from landing on Palestine's shores. From now on, all of our travels, by land or by boat, must be done in total secrecy in order to elude the British secret service.

Now it's December 1946 and we are finally ready to depart. But even *we* can't be allowed to know where we are going. All we know is that we will leave in the middle of the night in what look like military trucks covered with tarps. And we will do so in total silence.

We have traveled an entire night and day, only stopping in dense forests for food and bathroom breaks. Now it's night again, and at last the trucks have stopped at a gate guarded by a member of the Haganah (Jewish Defense Forces). A Hebrew word we can barely hear is used as a password.

We drive on and stop at an ornate building that looks like a mansion. Finally, we can get out of the trucks and stretch our legs.

Inside, we are assigned rooms. We are so exhausted that we just head for our beds and fall asleep. The next morning, some of us walk outside the building's walled grounds and see a sign on the gate that reads *Saint Jerome*.

After some more snooping, we find out that we are in Marseilles, France. We also get word that *Saint Jerome* is a former insane asylum. (I think to myself, *I should feel right at home here!*) Saint Jerome is used by the Haganah as temporary housing for groups that will board ships for Palestine.

So how long will we have to wait for a chance to board a ship? Nobody seems to know. In the meantime, we will resume our normal course of studies and activities. Apparently, we're even going to rehearse for a play that we are to put on.

Members from the Haganah will give us fitness exercises and judo lessons and a whole lot of martial arts training. They will also teach us how to act in case our ship gets boarded by the British as we reach the shores of Palestine. They will prepare us for all possible scenarios that may occur during a British interception of our boat.

It's now the first week of February 1947, and we've been here two long months. And then this evening, during a play rehearsal, we are told to be ready for departure in two hours– at 10:00 o'clock sharp. We are finally going to realize the centuries-old dream of our forefathers, the one they recited each year in their story of Passover: *"Leshana Habaa Bejerushalayim"* (Next year we will be in Jerusalem).

The trucks with their dimmed headlights have arrived exactly on time. We are all lined up and eager to go, but we have been instructed to be silent the rest of the trip in order not to attract any attention.

We're on our way, and I can't help but think how different *this* trip is from the trip I made with my father on the German truck from the Shrodula Ghetto to the Annaberg concentration camp. How I wish my father were with me now! Just thinking of all that has happened since that earlier transport makes my head spin.

Today, the trucks are covered on all sides by tarps, so no one can see in and we can't see out. The late hour and the jostling of the truck are making me so sleepy I don't think I can stay awake.

I *did* fall asleep, for how long I don't know. Lolek just shook me awake and said we have to get off the truck. It's still dark outside, but I can see that we are at the seashore, lining up to board a ship.

I ask where we are and learn that it is the town of Seth, a small Spanish fishing village just south of the French border. Here, the Haganah has a 750-ton fishing boat to ferry 750 enthusiastic youngsters to their Promised Land.

The line is moving very quickly now, because everybody knows that every minute counts. We have to get aboard before daybreak to avoid being discovered by British intelligence.

Oh, my God! Inside the ship we are packed onto bunks tighter than—well, you know—sardines. Members of the Haganah are in total charge of the operation. As soon as all of us were on board, we left port. We were all assembled under the deck to be given the following orders: No one is allowed on deck during daylight hours. Plastic barf bags are to be tied tightly after use and tossed into specified steel drums. Food and drinks will be served in pre-packed rations. All wrappings and disposable items must be deposited in specified containers. There are only three toilets each for boys and girls, so we must line up in an orderly fashion and avoid quarrels.

We were also told that the Aegean Sea can get very choppy during the winter, and many of us may get seasick and vomit. Those of us who aren't seasick must help those that are and maintain cleanliness and proper hygiene at all times.

We can't all be on deck at once. Instead, there will be a scheduled time for each group to be there during the night. Young people from many different Zionist movements are on this ship, ranging in their faith from the ultra orthodox to the secular, and in their politics from the far right to the far left. In other words, we are a mirror of Jewish society in Europe. Regardless of our views, we all share a common goal, and the spirits and enthusiasm of everyone aboard the ship are very high. We know that we are making a valiant stand and an important historical statement to the entire world: *We will no longer tolerate the spilling of Jewish blood. We want to be the masters of our own destiny in our ancestral land!* We will go to the Promised Land in spite of the blockades set up by the British Empire. We will do what it takes to exercise our right of return to our ancestral home.

After a couple of days on board, I must admit that this is not an easy journey. The ship is extremely crowded, and many of the kids are puking their guts out. Fortunately I don't suffer much from motion sickness, and I have arranged my schedule to sleep during the day so that I can go up on deck at night.

It feels great to be on deck with the stars reflecting on the water and the breeze blowing in my face. Some of us—even those with ocean sickness—dance the Horah and other folk dances on deck during all hours of the night. Nothing can keep me from enjoying every moment of the journey. I just keep thinking about our goal: reaching the shores of Palestine.

We are now 12 days into our voyage, and the Haganah is conducting meetings on the deck to prepare us for the critical moment when we reach Palestine. They tell us it is highly unlikely that we will not be detected by the British blockade. If we are lucky enough *not* to be detected, we will disembark from the ship as fast as we can as soon as it hits the sand on the shore. Then we are to run to the nearest kibbutz for shelter.

The most likely scenario, however, is that the British Navy will intercept our ship once it gets into the territorial waters about 12 miles from the shoreline. Naval ships will escort our ship to the port of Haifa, where they will forcefully board it. Then they will move all the passengers onto a British ship and take them to detention camps on the island of Cyprus.

When this happens, there is no point in resisting. Instead, we must all gather on the deck of the ship in a peaceful protest and sing the Hebrew National Anthem so the world can bear witness to the cruel ways in which the British are treating the survivors of the Holocaust.

It is the night of the fourteenth day of the voyage, and we can clearly see the lights on the shores of Palestine. We begin rejoicing at the sight when suddenly three British warships surround our ship and commandeer it to the port of Haifa. Since we were forewarned about this sequence of events, I quickly run down to my bunk to collect my belongings and run back onto the deck.

By the time I get back on deck, our ship is anchored and sailors of the British Navy are coming on board. All 750 of us are on deck standing at attention. As the British sailors reach the deck, we start singing the Hebrew National Anthem as the international media photograph and record the scene. Here we are singing a patriotic song, while the British use high-pressure water hoses to disperse us. Then they start forcing us onto their ships. I can't help but think that they have a lousy sense of public relations!

A fellow standing next to me who speaks English tells me what to say to the British soldier when he grabs me, and I, of course, am happy to oblige, even though I have no idea what I'm saying.

"You fucking bastard!" I yell.

His face turns red, and he shoves his rifle butt into my forehead. I figure that this would be a good time for me to faint, so I fall to the ground and lie still. I had hoped they might take me to the local hospital, but instead they pour a bucket of ice water on my head.

This certainly gets me up in a hurry, and they grab me and drag me onto their ship headed for Cyprus. This is the price I pay for my first English lesson!

A Brief Detour to Famagusta, Cyprus

Welcome to Cyprus, an island in the middle of nowhere. Our new home is a sprawling English military camp, which the British converted into a detention camp for thousands of Jewish Holocaust survivors at the end of World War II. This act by the British government was in total contradiction of the Balfour Declaration of November 2, 1917, in which the British Foreign Secretary, Sir Arthur James Balfour, declared that Great Britain would take a favorable view of the establishment of a Jewish National Home in Palestine. That was then, and this is now. The Arab countries of the Middle East oppose Jewish migration and settlement in Palestine. They have oil and the British want it, so to keep the sheiks happy they are willing to ignore their moral duty–despite all that we Jews suffered during the war.

Inside the British detention camps here, the "inmates" have one goal: the establishment of a Jewish national home in Palestine. While the British provide food, lodging and medical treatment, the camp activities are exclusively governed by the Haganah and the Irgun (an ultra right militant organization). In other words, the Zionists have total autonomy.

Here we are taught the practical necessities of daily life as pioneers in a hostile environment. Along with general high school subjects, we are given paramilitary training by members of the Haganah who were sent to Cyprus for this purpose. We are kept busy from dawn to dusk, and we have night exercises on top of it. Our daily routine begins with getting up at 6:00 a.m., having a five-mile jog followed by a 45-minute judo session and eating breakfast. Then we have normal school sessions during the day, with an hour break for lunch. School ends at 4:30 in the afternoon, giving us an hour and a half to do our homework. Dinner is served at 6:00 p.m.

At 7:00 p.m. we attend night orientation classes, where we are taught to navigate by the stars. We use tunnels that run underneath the barbed wire fence to get outside the camp. On our nightly excursions, several groups go for a few miles in different directions with the objective of meeting at a central point two hours later. It's a great exercise in familiarizing ourselves with night conditions in varied terrain. Our instructors tell us that there are many tactical advantages to night warfare.

After meeting all requirements of the training course, we were sworn in as members of the Haganah. We sat on the ground in a large dark tent. In front of us was a raised platform with a white curtain drawn across it, and behind the curtain was a table with three chairs where our military instructors were seated.

As they called each student for the swearing-in ceremony, you could see his or her shadow on the white curtain with a gun in the right hand and the palm of the left hand laid on the Bible. This was a very emotional moment for me. After the ceremony we built a fire and danced the night away, starting with the Horah and ending up with all sorts of folk dances. But the next morning at 6:00 sharp we got up for our jog, just as we did every day.

That morning, during the judo session the trainer had us lie down on the ground and then asked us to harden our stomach muscles. Then he jumped from belly to belly in his bare feet. This was very hard to take at first, but it sure has built up our belly muscles!

Our training just gets harder and harder. Now we have to navigate all sorts of obstacles like ravines and narrow rivers. In July we practiced crossing a river on ropes that stretched over a span of 50 feet at a height of 22 feet above the water. We had to crawl across the span with a pack on our backs and get off at the other end on a dangling rope.

I was unable to make it across to the end and let my feet dangle down, but then my instructor asked me to get my feet back up and make it across to the other end. I simply was not able to do it, so he finally asked me to jump down onto the ground. In the jump I fractured my left leg and was taken to the hospital in Famagusta, where they put my leg in a cast. All my buddies had a field day signing it, but I was "bummed," as I think you kids say, because I couldn't take part in all of the activities. So guess what I did: I took up stone carving during my spare time! Now don't laugh–I enjoyed it a lot, mostly because it helped pass the time quickly.

Well, guess what's happening now: apparently there's been a lot of pressure on the British government to ease some of the restrictions on the Holocaust survivors in the camps here. And so her Majesty, the Queen of England, will now allow 500 orphaned Holocaust survivors to immigrate to Palestine. Because I have a fractured leg, *I* have been chosen to be among the 500! We are scheduled to leave for Palestine by the twenty-third of August. While waiting, my cast was taken off, but I'm still on the departure list.

Can you imagine–I'll actually be in the Promised Land for my 18th birthday. It's the best birthday gift I could ever think of. I can't wait to leave!

On the evening of the twenty-second of August, we are informed that our entire group will be able to join the transport to Palestine tomorrow morning. Of course we are overjoyed at the news. Tonight we won't sleep–we'll just celebrate and dance.

In the wee hours of the morning, the party breaks up and we quickly gather our belongings and line up for the trip. As we line up, we notice that various other groups are going on the trip too. Eitan, our trainer from the Haganah, is with us and asks us to listen up. He tells us that there are major discussions in the international community about establishing a Jewish national home in Palestine. He explains that this is a very crucial time for us. The news is so exciting that we spend the rest of our time in line talking about nothing else.

At the port of Famagusta, we are met by an army of photographers and newspaper people from the British and international press. They are here to publicize the act of generosity by her Majesty the Queen of England in allowing 500 orphans of the Holocaust to go to Palestine. We, of course, just want to board the ship and get on our way. When the anchors are finally lifted and the ship is in motion, we all start to cheer.

To our surprise, the British soldiers on this ship are very nice and polite, serving food and passing out goodies as we make our way to the shores of Palestine. But we have only one interest—the goal we have worked so hard to attain.

Our group of orphans in a photo taken after we reached Negba. I am the second from the left in the second row.

As soon as we see land, all 500 of us go up on the deck to witness the moment. Yes, there's the Haifa harbor and, above it, the majestic Mount Carmel.

As soon as we drop anchor and the ship stops moving, we all stand at attention and burst out singing the *Hatikvah* (the Israeli national anthem). It is one of the most memorable moments of my life, and tears of joy run down my cheeks.

On the bus ride south to Negba, the kibbutz where we will live, our Haganah trainer points out various towns: Tel Aviv, Jaffa, Rechovot. An hour and 45 minutes later we arrive.

Life in Negba

The people who live here on the Negba kibbutz are secular in their beliefs and socialist in their politics. But in the Holy Land, it doesn't matter what views you have; most people live in communes. The reason for this is the need for safety in numbers, because there are many Arabs who want to harm us. For the same reason, most people who live on a kibbutz are strong supporters of the Haganah, although those in the far right movement rely for their protection on the Irgun.

Negba is located between the main highway leading from Tel Aviv to Gaza on the west and the crossroad leading from Gaza to Jerusalem on the east. The police compound known as Iraq El Suidan, which was built by the British, is located on a hill above us. The station serves to enforce the rules of the British mandate, and we at Negba are careful to maintain a cooperative relationship with the police there.

Negba is a self-contained agricultural kibbutz, whose members are hard-working idealists pursuing the Zionist goal. They all came from Eastern European countries. Our arrival will bring new blood to the place, and in order to make sure we fit in from the start we have been assigned a first-rate teaching staff. Here, our days are split between study, work and military training. One of our classes is an accelerated course in Hebrew language and literature, intended to help us communicate with the locals. Our work is in the fields and cow stables.

Military training here is absolutely essential because of the threats made by many leaders of neighboring Arab countries, as well as by the Grand Mufti of Jerusalem. We train together with the boys and girls who were born in and around Negba, and this will help us become integrated.

Despite our hectic schedule, we try to keep up with local as well as international news. We are especially interested in the talks taking place in the newly formed United Nations Assembly in New York. That body is considering Resolution 181, which would establish a Jewish and an Arab state side by side in Palestine.

The Jewish community all over the world and the Zionist organizations in particular are fully aware that the western world now feels guilty for standing idly by while six million Jews were killed, but that their guilt will only last a short while. So now is the time for us to ask them to right the wrong that was done to us. Now is the time to ask them to vote for the establishment of a Jewish national home. Now is the time the newspapers and radio broadcasts are keeping the topic alive in front of the entire world. For us, it's now or never.

While all of this was going on, I fell in love. Her name is Gilah Davidowicz and she lives here on the kibbutz. Gilah is really a very attractive girl. She has short black hair, glowing black eyes and an amazing figure. She's from a Hungarian family, but she lost her parents during the war.

Gilah carries a great deal of pain from the loss of her family and has a fierce dedication to our cause. We first met in the orphanage, but in the beginning we really didn't take to each other. Little by little, though, I began to really *look* at her and get to know her, and the rest, as they say, is history.

Like me, Gilah is a trained fighter, and she commands a great deal of respect from the people around here. It would not be going too far to say that she is a very wise person. Gilah is my companion in the trenches, where we are both assigned to position #5 on the edge of the kibbutz. (The entire perimeter of Negba is divided into defensive positions. Number 5 is under my command and consists of Gilah, two other boys, and me.)

Shmilek (me) at age 19 and my girlfriend Gilah Davidovitz

When we have a few minutes to ourselves, Gila and I often talk about our deepest beliefs. We have agreed that in our hearts we know that we will stand and fight like tigers to defend the right of our people to live free in our ancestral homeland. Never again will Jews go like sheep to the slaughterhouse. We will help see to that.

Gilah is really my first girlfriend, and I guess you would say, "What took you so long?" But, dear reader, did you see any opportunities for me to meet girls in the concentration camps or to have a normal teenage life at all?

Now that I've fallen in love with Gilah, it's not as if we can go on dates. Instead, we have our military training together and steal a few minutes each day to kiss and—what do you call it?—*pet* when we're not busy with our education and work and military maneuvers. But I love her fiercely and hope that I never have to be parted from her. Some day, when our people's troubles are over, I want to marry her.

At last a United Nations vote on the establishment of a Jewish state is set for today, November 29, 1947. What a historic moment! Here in Palestine, there has been dancing and singing all over the place for days. And of course there's a lot of excitement among Jews everywhere.

At the kibbutz, preparations are being made for us to listen to the United Nations deliberations and vote in our large mess hall. Right after dinner, the dining tables were put along the walls and chairs were set up in rows. From what I've heard on the radio, Jewish communities throughout the world will be glued to their radios to listen to the deliberations. Here, there is a 10-hour time difference, so we may have to stay up all night to hear the results.

It is finally dawn here, and the voting is finished. The final results are 33 in favor, 13 against and 10 abstentions on the resolution to establish a Jewish and an Arab state side by side in Palestine. Everyone here is going crazy, dancing and singing and jumping up and down with joy.

The sad part of the vote is that all the Arab countries rejected the idea. They made it clear that they do not want a Jewish state at all. This means that we are now facing threats from the north, south and east, as well as within Palestine itself from the forces of the Grand Mufti of Jerusalem.

So what are the next steps? It will now be left up to the Jewish National Council to meet with the British and set up a date when the British will transfer power and the new state will be born.

Months have passed, and the date set for the transfer of power is tomorrow, May 15, 1948. This means that the British will have to leave all their bases by midnight tonight. The question now is, what condition will the country be in when the British leave?

In the weeks and months after the UN vote, the British, who are supposed to be completely neutral, have made it very clear that they favor the Arabs over the Jews. They have transferred to the Arabs all the strategic locations between Tel Aviv and Jerusalem and between Gaza and Jerusalem. To give one example, they handed the Arabs the Latrun Police Station, which controls the roads from Tel Aviv to Jerusalem. That means we will be denied access to our own Jewish capital. Not only that—the British have left all their weapons and

145

ammunition in Latrun and other police stations so the Arabs can use them to kill Jews.

Why are they doing this? Because the British want all the oil concessions they can get from the Arabs, so they are giving them an enormous advantage. You see, all of the Arab countries that surround us, and the Grand Mufti of Jerusalem, have vowed to drive us into the ocean. Right after the UN vote was taken, hostilities started in various areas, as the Arabs tried to find weaknesses in our defenses.

We haven't just stood idly by, either. In Negba we took frantic measures to prepare ourselves for an attack. We built a chain of trenches and bunkers. We erected barbed wire fences. We learned to use Molotov cocktails and hand grenades. We prepared to plant mines in the ground in front of our fences in case of an infantry attack.

The problem is that while the surrounding Arab countries are arming themselves, we Jews are prevented by the rules of the British mandate from importing any weapons or ammunition. This puts us at a great disadvantage and forces us to concentrate on other defensive

Here we are training to defend Negba.

measures in the hope that we can hold back Arab attacks until we are able to declare our independence.

In the meantime, the Haganah and the worldwide Zionist organization have purchased weapons and ammunition from around the world, to arrive in the Jewish state right after the declaration of independence. Needless to say, we have been too busy to continue with our school work.

The Jewish State Is Attacked and My World Falls Apart

As we suspected, the Egyptians didn't wait for the official declaration of independence. Their air force attacked us, dropped incendiary bombs on our haystacks and strafed our cow stables, killing several cows. We got the message and immediately sent the young children away from this combat zone and into the interior of the country.

Tomorrow is Saturday, May 15th, the Jewish Sabbath, so in respect for the religious feelings of many who fear desecrating a holy day, the Jewish Council of Palestine has decided to make the declaration of independence before sundown today.

Now we sit in complete silence as David Ben-Gurion, the leader of the Council, proclaims the establishment of an independent Jewish state. As he finishes speaking, we all stand at attention and sing the Israeli national anthem. I hug Gilah and am so happy to share with her this historical moment in our lives. Tears of happiness are running down our cheeks.

The formal declaration of a Jewish state hasn't fazed the Egyptians. They have urged the Arab residents of Palestine to leave their homes for a short time, while the Egyptians achieve victory. Then, they say, the Arabs can return home and share in the loot that has been taken from the defeated Jewish residents.

The Egyptians aren't the only ones who think this way. The British are also sure that 650,000 Jews could not possibly hold back many millions of Arabs. After all, we Jews have our backs to the Mediterranean Sea, and we're being attacked by an overwhelming combined force of all the Arab armies—Syria and Lebanon from the north, Transjordan with the Arab Legion from the east, Iraq and Egypt from the south. Common sense would dictate that there is no way the Jews could survive such an onslaught.

As a matter of fact the Arabs have made stunning gains within the first few days of their invasion. The Arab Legion of Transjordan was able to cut Jerusalem off from the rest of the country. The Egyptian army cut off the entire Negev Desert right at the crossroads above us and occupied the police station of Iraq El Suidan. The Syrians and Lebanese in the north were pushing southward. It's a pretty bleak picture but not one that can dampen our spirits and determination.

Negba has been the target of Egyptian airplanes, which have attacked us daily. All we can do is dig deeper into our trenches. When the Egyptians occupied Gaza and went north along the coast, we were concerned that we too might get cut off. After all, they attacked and took over the kibbutz of Yad Mordechai, which is northeast of Gaza, and we knew that we were next. To protect us, the Haganah sent an expeditionary force and tried one night to attack and take over the police station, but with no success. The reason for a night attack was simple—we have a very small force with limited firepower, but at night we are able to place loud speakers and sparklers in different spots to give the illusion of a large force, and we can take advantage of an element of surprise that would not be possible in daylight. On the second of June, the Egyptians shelled our positions for six hours solid. Their planes flew several sorties over our heads, strafing the entire area with a blanket of fire. Then they sent 20 tanks towards our positions, shelling us from their turrets all the while.

But as soon as they came over our minefields, their tanks got disabled and they were forced to retreat. We lost six of our soldiers in that attack, while they left over a hundred bodies strewn all over the battlefield and our minefields.

We learned important lessons from this encounter. First, don't open fire until their infantry reaches our minefields. Second, be ready to use hand grenades and Molotov cocktails only after they breach our fences. Why? Because we have very limited ammunition and must use it in the most effective way possible.

We also realized that the Egyptian soldiers are not motivated to fight for the Palestinians and give up their lives for them. And we witnessed a gross lack of communication between the attacking forces and their commanders. Sometimes it reminded us of a Keystone Kops movie, because their artillery fire kept exploding on their own troops and killing them.

The first battle tested our ability to hold our positions and repel the attacking forces. We have to be fully prepared for more attacks to follow.

Tonight is the fifth of June, and here in our bunker I am taking a short nap while Gilah stands guard duty on top of the trench. Suddenly, the thud of an enemy artillery shell jars me awake, and I start yelling for Gilah to take cover. But it is too late. The shell explodes right in front of our trench and Gilah is hit by shrapnel.

I can tell she has been badly wounded and immediately call the medics, who rush her to the first aid station, but again it is too late. Within minutes, she is dead. The medics tell me that her aorta was severed and she bled to death.

There is no time to grieve. The Egyptians are pounding our position with a steady barrage of artillery fire, and the sky above us is buzzing with flickering shells that are falling and exploding all around us. As the skies start to get light, we see hundreds of enemy tanks rolling from the police station towards us.

We immediately phone our commanders to inform them of the situation on the ground. They order us to stay calm and under cover as we watch the tanks advance. We are not to open fire on them until after their infantry units have entered the minefields just outside our fence.

Now, everything is in a state of chaos. I hear explosions all over the battlefield, and the air is filled with the smell of gunpowder. For some unknown reason, the Egyptians are shelling *their own* troops on *our* minefields, so we can't tell if those troops are dying from the shelling or from our mines or from our machine guns. It is a scene from the bowels of Hell.

While all of this is going on, the Egyptian tanks keep pressing forward, moving towards our perimeter even as they roll over their own wounded soldiers. One of the Egyptian tanks breaks through our fence at position #6, about 75 feet to the left of our position.

The crew of position #6 tosses a few Molotov cocktails on the tank and it ignites. The heat of the burning steel causes the men in the tank to jump out of its escape hutch, and when they do they are mowed down by our crew. The battle is very intense and I am pumped up with adrenalin. Only when I wipe the sweat off my forehead do I see that it is red and realize that I've been injured. Gingerly, I try to take my helmet off, and as I do I feel a sharp pain. Apparently, shrapnel hit the helmet, causing a sharp edge to puncture my scalp.

Clearly, there's no way I can leave the battlefield, so I call in a medic, who bandages me up. While he is doing this, all the explosions suddenly stop and everything is still. We glance up and exchange a look, wondering what has happened. And then we see the strangest sight: on the battlefield, all of the tanks are retreating, leaving the dead and injured behind on the scorched earth.

Later we learn that the Egyptian losses numbered 400, while ours numbered 10, including Gilah. In addition to the dead bodies, the Egyptians left behind some of their injured soldiers on our minefields.

This was hard to watch, because we couldn't help them. It was too risky for our medics to go into the minefields.

Now we had to bury our dead defenders. Gilah and two other comrades from the kibbutz were placed in a common grave for "the brave defenders of Negba." The others were sent to their families.

In the days since then, the pain and sorrow of losing Gilah has gotten worse and worse. I keep wondering if there is anything I could have done to prevent it. Now I am tortured by the same feelings of guilt I had when I lost my father. Is this a product of age-old Judeo-Christian teaching? Are guilt feelings so deeply rooted in our traditions that we allow them to ruin our lives? Will I ever be free of them?

A Welcome Cease-Fire

In the aftermath of the big battle, we have time to evaluate our actions during our fight for survival. We are proud that we were able to repulse an enemy attack against such great odds. Nevertheless, this is an extremely difficult period for the nation as a whole. Unless a miracle takes place, I can't see how we will last.

That miracle has come in the form of a United Nations cease-fire, which took effect as of the eleventh of June. During the cease-fire, weapons and ammunition that have been donated by Jewish and Christian organizations around the world are arriving in Israeli ports.

Czechoslovakia is one of the countries that is supplying us with modern machine guns and armaments and—get this—they are from the factories that the Germans left behind during the war! But while most of the world is sympathetic to our success and our survival, the British government is still trying to keep military equipment from getting into our hands.

During the cease-fire, I will have a one-week furlough from my duties to make a trip to Jerusalem to visit a second cousin, Zemach Silberberg, who lives there. (Until now, no civilian traffic between Jerusalem and the rest of the country has been allowed.) Before I go, I will pick a crate of tomatoes to take as a gift.

For weeks, I have mailed all my letters to Mother from Tel Aviv so she wouldn't think I was in a war zone. In this next letter I can talk

153

about my trip to Jerusalem, though sadly I won't be able to report a visit to my grandfather's' grave on the Mount of Olives. That section of Jerusalem and the Old City and Holy places are in the hands of the Arab Legions of Transjordan.

Well, the trip has been quite an adventure. First, I had to go to Rechovot, where the convoy for the trip to Jerusalem joined the military escort. There, I was assigned to one of the supply trucks in the convoy.

The troops who were escorting us were standing on the truck's running board, ready to jump off and take defensive positions in case of attack, and we ourselves were armed with rifles and belts of hand grenades. Once we reached the winding road in total darkness, the trucks in the convoy were not allowed to turn on their headlights, so we literally crawled the rest of the night. It wasn't until dawn that we connected again with the main road to Jerusalem.

Now I'm finally in Jerusalem, and right away I am impressed by the architecture of the buildings. Most of them are constructed of native yellow stone carved out of the hills that surround the city. As the morning sun hits the buildings, they give off a golden glow.

Shortly after I arrive I find my cousin's house, and it's not long before I realize that he is an ultra-orthodox Chasidic Jew. Right off the bat, he lets me know that he finds my secular beliefs obnoxious, but fortunately we agree to disagree and not to engage in discussions of religion or politics.

My main reason for coming here is to find out how my beloved grandfather died in 1942. I remember him praying at the hospital for my recovery when my appendix burst. I remember the going-away party in the fall of 1938 that was given in his honor. I remember the Kaddish that Father was saying to honor him when I escaped from the Death March. Even though I'm not a believer, I attribute the success of that escape to his, you might say, *divine* intervention. It's just sad that I can't pay my respects at his gravesite.

When I get back to Negba, I learn that many members of the Palmach (special forces) unit were called in for a special action in Hertzlia, a town north of Tel Aviv. Their mission was to prevent the ship *Altalena* from unloading its cargo of weapons and ammunition, which was destined for the right-wing military organization Irgun. Israel's leader, David Ben-Gurion, recently declared that Haganah is the only military force responsible for the security of the country.

The crew of the *Altalena* left the ship, and its cargo was unloaded for use by the Israeli defense forces. I'm relieved. If things had gone the other way, we might have found ourselves in the middle of a civil war. That Ben-Gurion is one wise man!

The cease-fire has been going on for a while now, and the state of Israel has used it very effectively. As soon as large shipments of weapons and military equipment arrive in our ports, they are immediately distributed to crucial battlefield areas across Israel. During the entire cease-fire, we have smuggled weapons and supplies to Negev. In the darkness of night, our scouts lead convoys of soldiers carrying weapons and ammunition through enemy lines to get here. It helps that we are trained for night warfare and are familiar with the terrain. Here in the kibbutz, we are learning how to use the new machine guns, the three-inch mortar equipment and advanced communication equipment.

Looking back at the mess we found ourselves in before the first cease-fire, I can't help but wonder how we were ever able to repel an attack of such overwhelming force. The answer to this in simple Hebrew is *Ein Breira* (No Alternative), but is it really as simple as that? True, we had no alternative but to fight for our right to have a place in the sun, but there was more to it. We had just survived the Holocaust. We were carrying the burden of 2,000 years of Jewish persecution on our shoulders. We had the courage of our convictions and could endure whatever we needed to. We were determined to show the world *yes, we can do it!*

And look at the Arabs who fought us. These poor soldiers are really nothing more than slaves, serving corrupt rulers who deny them their basic rights and freedoms as human beings and citizens. For this reason, they lack will, determination and, most of all, a reason to fight a war that has been forced on them.

Boy have things been hopping around here! On the eighth of July, the Jordanian forces of the Arab Legion broke the cease-fire and we went on the offensive. The Arab armies had isolated the Negev Desert and Jerusalem, and now the Israeli defense forces mounted attacks to regain control of the crossroads that separate the Negev Desert from the rest of Israel.

The operation succeeded after several hours of intensive fighting, and by the time the United Nations declared the second cease-fire we were in control of the crossroads that united the country. But in the process our side suffered enormous losses.

Now there is no doubt that we have the upper hand on the ground, and it's only a question of time before the remaining pockets of resistance are cleared up.

My Dreams Are Shattered—or Are They?

Life in Negba is back to normal. The children and the staff have returned to the kibbutz. The fields and livestock are being attended to as usual. And there is a lot of rebuilding to be done. The concrete water tower is riddled with holes and can no longer be used. Homes and cow stables are damaged and need to be repaired. The list goes on.

Harder to repair is the void in my heart left by Gilah's death.

The kibbutz has also returned to its normal schedule of meetings to discuss issues affecting its members. One such issue involves deciding which children to send to college.

Now I fully understand that the kibbutz does not have enough funds to send all its children to college, but the idea of taking a vote on such a sensitive matter makes me question the whole idea of a communal system. I have given the issue a lot of thought in the last few days and have come to the conclusion that if *I* had children of college age, I would not want someone else to decide if they are worthy of going to college.

This question has soured my whole attitude towards communal living and has made me have second thoughts about whether I want to continue being here. Winston Churchill has said, "If you are not an idealist at the age of 18, you have no heart. If you are an idealist at the age of 40, you have no brain." Well, I have devoted a lot of energy to idealistic causes and have given kibbutz life a chance, but now I wonder if it is really the way I want to spend the rest of my life. Maybe I am better suited to making my way in a competitive, free-enterprise society. Maybe I need to test the waters and work for myself.

After talking with some of my friends here on the kibbutz, I realize that I'm not the only one who is questioning the utopian ideas on which communal life is based. In fact, there are five of us who want to branch out and try something new. We've talked about setting up a construction company that specializes in building standardized, poured-concrete, 50-head cow barns. There's a lot more planning to do before we can set ourselves up in business, but I think it will work.

We've started to flesh things out and decided that our work should be based on a three-day schedule. On the first day of each job, we'll set up the forms and rebar. Early on the second day we'll pour the concrete. On the third day we'll dismantle the forms and load them on a truck ready for the next job. It will be a standardized system that should work quite well. And as the country's population grows, there should be more and more demand for our services.

And so, with a new goal for my life, I will leave the kibbutz–I hope on good terms with everyone.

It is now 1952, and I've been pursuing my dream of being in business for over two years. My friends and I have had to work from dawn to dusk every single day, and we've been able to save some money. In my case, I wanted to use it to buy a bit of property, build a house and eventually settle down here. Sounds good, huh?

Unfortunately my dreams were recently shot down overnight. You see, Israel's finance minister, Dov Joseph, suddenly decided to revamp the country's financial system and devalue its money, the shekel, by 90 percent. One day my money was worth something, the next day it was worthless.

Because of this idiot's actions, we had to dissolve our corporation and stop work on our projects. Two and a half years of hard work, and I have nothing to show for it.

Now I am living temporarily in the home of my cousins, the Poisson family, in Ramat Gan, a suburb of Tel Aviv. I am very thankful for their generosity in accepting me as part of their family. For the time being I have taken a job as a framing carpenter with a local construction company, but I plan to leave Israel soon.

You see my mother now lives in the United States, and she's been after me to visit her. I finally decided to give in, but getting a visa to enter the country has taken over six months. First I had to get my Israeli passport, and then I had to wait my turn to get a US visa to enter the United States.

Mother and Aunt Sarah have arranged for me to fly to Rome in July. Then I will visit with my aunt in Zeilsheim, Germany, return to Italy and sail from the port of Naples to the United States on an Italian ship called *Conte Biancamano*.

So what does the future hold for me? So far, I have learned that people can be unbelievably cruel, but they can also be wonderfully kind. I've lived through one of the worst horrors in the history of the world and survived. I've lost most of my family and the love of my life and had my heart broken over and over. Yet I've found that I'm smart and can take on challenges I would never have thought possible. What choice do I have but to start my new life–perhaps in America–with a determination to succeed, no matter what curve balls life throws at me? What choice do *any of us* have, when it comes right down to it?

And so I bid you *shalom*, my friend. Go in peace and live your life well.

Epilogue

In 1952 I sailed to New York City on the *Conte Biancamano* and visited my mother as I decided what to do with my life. There I enrolled in the Morgenthaler Linotype School, a first step in continuing the family tradition of working in printing. After graduation, I took a job as a linotype operator in Clyde, Ohio, because I wanted to be in a place where English was pretty much the only language spoken. I hoped that once my English was better, I could attend the Rochester Institute of Technology and earn a BS in printing. (To maintain my visa status in the United States, I had to enroll in an accredited college.) Although my first application to RIT was rejected, I was later admitted to the college. After graduating, I worked as a production manager for several printing and publishing companies in New York. I also bought up old, dilapidated row houses, know as brownstones, and completely renovated them—sometimes bringing fine craftsmen over from Europe to work on them. That venture earned me a feature story in the *New York Times*.

During my long career in New York, I held bitter memories of growing up in Polish ghettos and labor camps and later finding out that my brothers and sister and many other family members had been brutally tortured and murdered at Auschwitz-Birkenau Concentration Camp. Worst of all, I bore a heavy burden of guilt for escaping from the Blechhammer Death March without my father. All I wanted to do was forget my memories and forget Poland.

Photo of the war memorial at Blechhammer camp (taken in 2007 by Jacques Lahitte and reused with permission)

Then in the year 2000, I changed my mind. By then I was retired, and at the urging of family and friends I was thinking about writing my memoirs. And so I contacted a friend, John Miller, who had worked at Pergamon Press when I was running the company's in-house print shop. Would John consider accompanying me to Poland and visiting the places where I had spent the years of my youth? "I would be honored," he replied, and in May of 2000 we found ourselves in Warsaw, Poland, ready to begin the journey into my past.

I wish I could say that we found things in Poland changed for the better. I wish I could report that Jews are welcome there and that World War II improved our treatment once and for all. But that would be a lie.

When John and I visited Auschwitz-Birkenau—now a World Heritage site—I was heartened by the vast displays of photographs and artifacts that told the true story of the horrifying things that were done to my people there. But when John and I stopped in the cafeteria for lunch, I was standing in front of the counter studying the menu on the wall when I heard the boy behind the counter say, "Well hurry up and make up your mind, *Jew!*" Nothing had changed.

When we visited my hometown of Jaworzno, I was in for another shock. I was excited to see the old family home and hoped to be allowed to go inside. But when I knocked on the door and told the present owner who I was, I was told, "No." Nothing had changed.

For years, it had galled me that our house—and the houses of other local Jews—had been given to new families as soon as we were sent to the ghetto *with no compensation to us, the original owners.* So before we left Poland, I met with a lawyer in Krakow and began proceedings to reclaim our house, which by rights of inheritance was now mine. My plan was to give the house to the City of Jaworzno, but on my own terms.

To make a long story short, the lawyer *sounded* helpful and sympathetic to my plight. He certainly was willing to take my money! And I *did* appear in the courts of Jaworzno, where the present owner testified that my mother had given him the property for saving her life (!) and his son-in-law made several blatant anti-Semitic remarks, which the judge carefully ignored. Even when the son-in-law looked at me and said, "Too bad Hitler didn't finish the job!" the judge did not intervene.

Still my lawyer promised me that everything would be taken care of and I would have my property in short order. So I returned to the United States and waited. After ten years passed with no progress whatsoever, I fired him and hired another attorney, but nothing has happened.

The reception I got in Poland depressed me, but there were some wonderful exceptions—two women in Jaworzno who befriended us and helped me deal with the local bureaucracy, the young waitress at our hotel, who took a great interest in my story, and several people who testified on my behalf in court.

In 2011 I self-published my memoirs in a version intended for adult readers. It is called *From Hell to the Promised Land* and is available from Amazon. In 2012 I published *What Made Sammy Run?* for teens.

Glossary

These terms were used but not defined in text:

Anti-Aircraft Battery–a grouping of heavy guns used to shoot down enemy planes.

Cheder *(KHEY-duhr)*–a religious school where Jewish children learn Hebrew and study prayer books and the Jewish holy book, the Torah.

Hebrew–the ancient language of the Jews. It is now the official language of Israel, but elsewhere it is only used for sacred occasions, not daily conversation.

Jewish High Holy Days–Rosh Hashanah and Yom Kippur, which occur within a 10-day period in September or October (see definitions below).

Kaddish *(KAHD-ish)*–a hymn of praise to God, recited either as part of a daily religious service or in honor of someone who has died.

Kiddush *(KI-doosh* or *Ki-DOOSH)*–a blessing recited over wine and bread the evening before the Sabbath or a festival.

Kaiser Wilhelm–the last emperor of Germany, beginning in 1888.

Orthodox Jew–one who strictly follows the traditions and ceremonies of Judaism.

Passover–a Jewish holiday of seven or eight days that celebrates the ancient deliverance of Jews from slavery in Egypt. It occurs in April, near the time of Easter.

Promised Land–roughly, the land now occupied by Israel. According to the Hebrew Bible (in Genesis, Exodus and Deuteronomy), it was the land of Canaan, given by God to the Israelites (the Jewish people), who are the descendants of Abraham, Isaac and Jacob. Opinions vary as to the exact location of its borders.

Rosh Hashana–the Jewish New Year, which falls in September or October and is celebrated for either one or two days with family gatherings, special meals and sweet foods. The dates of Rosh Hashana change as the Jewish calendar changes from year to year.

Synagogue *(SIN-a-gog)*–a Jewish place of worship.

Torah *(TOR-uh)*–the Jewish holy book, written on a parchment scroll, which contains the first five books of the Bible and a collection of writings covering Jewish law and religious law.

Yiddish–the daily language of orthodox Jews in Europe. Yiddish is an old Germanic dialect that is written using the Hebrew alphabet.

Yom Kippur–the Day of Atonement for sins committed against God. On this day, Jews do not work, but pray, meditate and fast (drink and eat nothing) for a 25-hour period.

The Nazi Camps

The camps to which Jews and many others (Gypsies, the mentally and physically incompetent, homosexuals, Jehovah's Witnesses and others) were taken had many different names, which reflected their purpose.

Concentration camps were built by the Germans to hold people they considered to be enemies of the state or subhuman (see above). Examples include Auschwitz, Dachau and Buchenwald camps.

Extermination camps (which the Nazis called *killing centers*) were built specifically as places to carry out mass murders of Jews and other "undesirable people" by gassing them. When prisoners arrived in the camps, they were told to undress, leave their valuables behind, and take showers to remove lice from their bodies. The "showers" sprayed the room with poisonous Zyklon B gas, and soon all the prisoners were dead. Then, after any gold fillings were removed from their mouths, their bodies were burned in huge ovens or buried in mass graves.

Death camps included extermination camps, where large groups were killed by poisonous gas, and camps where prisoners were so badly treated that they died of starvation, disease and other "natural" causes.

Labor camps were places where able-bodied males like Sam and his father were taken. There they were used on construction projects that furthered the German war effort. As long as a prisoner was healthy he was allowed to live, but anyone who got sick was taken to the infirmary and injected with cyanide poison and their bodies were cremated.

Discussion Questions
From Sam

1. When you read about my father and me, do you agree more with my impulsiveness and risk taking or with my father's cautiousness and failure to act? Think of some specific examples from the book.

2. For me, being able to think and act quickly when faced with new dangers and problems was a matter of life and death. Can you recall one or two examples of my ability to do so?

3. My feelings about God were very different from my father's. Do you recall what those feelings were?

4. When I escaped from the Death March without knowing if my father had followed me, do you think I was being driven by fear or selfishness? Why?

5. Do you remember the Mitzvahs (good deeds) that I did when I was a kid? Do you remember the Mitzvah I did because my parents asked me to? Why do you think they let their son take such terrible risks?

6. I obviously had mixed feelings about my father. Can you remember some examples of arguments we had and compare them to the disagreements today's teenagers have with their parents? Do you see similarities? Differences?

7. You'd think that in World War II, all Germans were bad and all Jews were good. I didn't find that to be true. Do you remember when and why I came to that conclusion?

8. What kept me from trying to escape when I was in the concentration camps, and what made me escape from the Death March?

9. As each of us grows to adulthood, we must choose how we will live our lives. Would you choose to live like me or like my father? Is there a middle ground?

10. If you were imprisoned the way I was, would you choose self-preservation over helping your fellow prisoners? Why?

11. At the train station as I was leaving for Hungary to become a freedom fighter in the Holy Land, I lashed out at my mother, who didn't want me to go. I said, "Look, Mom, maybe you could afford to lose a husband and three children, but I don't want that to happen to me! I must do something about it!" What would *you* have said in this situation? Would you have left your mother after having been parted from her for so long during the war?

12. When I got to Hungary, I learned the value of the education I missed during my years in the concentration camps. Can you understand why a good education was so important to me? How do you feel about the value of your own schooling?

13. In my book, the Nazis aren't the only ones who mistreat Jews. Talk about specific instances of prejudice that I encountered before and after the war. What is your reaction?

14. Today, we talk a lot about "bullying." Why do you think some classmates bully others? What parallels do you see between modern-day bullying and the prejudices I faced as a young Jew in German-controlled Poland? Can bullying ever be stopped, or is it an inborn human trait?

15. What are some things that are going on in the Middle East now, and how do you feel about Israel's actions in the region?

16. We all have fascinating stories to tell. Think about your own life, your family and your views about good and evil, right and wrong. Think about writing your own story. I'd love to read it!

Suggested Projects

If you are interested in learning more about Sam's world–perhaps for extra credit–here are some research topics you might want to pursue:

1. How does the Jewish calendar differ from our calendar? What are the major Jewish holidays, and when do they occur?

2. What were some of the major concentration, labor and extermination camps? Where were they located? What were the differences between them?

3. Develop a 1-2 page report on ghettos. What were they? Why did they exist? What was life like there?

4. Write about the Warsaw Ghetto uprising.

5. Write a report on the Auschwitz-Birkenau concentration camp. Include photographs.

6. Read the following account of anti-Semitism that Sam wrote and write a short paper on one aspect of it–the Romans driving Jews out of Israel 2,000 years ago, accusations that Jews were responsible for Christ's death, accusations that Jews were responsible for the Bubonic Plague and so on.

   Why do they hate us? You might well ask. Jews have lived in Europe ever since the Romans drove us out of Israel nearly 2,000 years ago, but in some ways we have never really fit in. For one thing, we don't share the Christian belief that Jesus is the Son of God. To us, he was a good but ordinary man, not the powerful leader that ancient scripture promised us. This belief–or lack of belief–led some churches, particularly the Roman Catholic Church, to preach that Jews rather than Romans were responsible for Christ's death. The fact is, crucifixion was a standard form of Roman punishment in Christ's time, but that doesn't seem to matter to those who are determined to hate us.

   Later, other wild accusations were made about us. One was that Jews caused the Bubonic Plague, which killed thousands of Europeans during the Middle Ages. (Now, of course, we know it was fleas, which were carried by rats.) Another accusation was that Jews led to Germany's defeat in the First World War (this despite the fact that many German Jews fought for their country in that war).

This went on for centuries. Jews were tortured and killed during the Spanish Inquisition of the 1400s and the pogroms organized in the 1800s in Russia and Poland. Early on in Europe, Jews were not allowed to hold certain jobs, for example farming, and as a result they gradually became merchants and bankers. Many of our people were very successful in these fields, which angered many non-Jews, who are known as gentiles.

But the worst anti-Semite was Adolph Hitler, who preached that Jews are an inferior, subhuman race that might taint the German "master race" through inter-marriage. He believed that we Jews must all be wiped from the face of the earth.

Sam Silberberg is now retired from a career in the printing industry in New York and lives with his wife Anita in Laguna Woods, California. His oral history has been taken by the Shoah Foundation, founded by Steven Spielberg, and his story is preserved by the United States Holocaust Memorial Museum in Washington, D.C. He often speaks to school, university and museum audiences.

Carolyn Buan, also retired, was the owner of Writing & Editing Services in Portland, Oregon for 20 years, writing, co-authoring and editing numerous publications, including several books on various aspects of Oregon history. She also taught high school English in Anchorage, Alaska.